PARABLES FOR THE THEATER

PARABLES FOR THE THEATER

TWO PLAYS BY BERTOLT BRECHT

The Good Woman of Setzuan

AND

The Caucasian Chalk Circle

ENGLISH VERSIONS BY ERIC AND MAJA BENTLEY

UNIVERSITY OF MINNESOTA PRESS • MINNEAPOLIS

London • Geoffrey Cumberlege • Oxford University Press

ALSO BY BERTOLT BRECHT

The Private Life of the Master Race
The Trial of Lucullus
Selected Poems

ALSO BY ERIC BENTLEY

A Century of Hero-Worship
The Playwright as Thinker
Bernard Shaw

PRINTED AT THE NORTH CENTRAL PUBLISHING COMPANY, ST. PAUL

BERTOLT BRECHT is perhaps the most remarkable German writer to come forward since the death of Franz Kafka some twenty-four years ago. Born in 1898, he served in the First World War and in his late teens wrote an antiwar poem that circulated orally in the German army and subsequently became famous — "The Ballad of the Dead Soldier." Before he was thirty he had won the Kleist Prize for his first notable play, *Drums in the Night*, published an astonishing first book of poems, *Sermons for the Home*, and completed a version of "The Beggar's Opera" which summed up a whole epoch in European culture. From 1933 to 1941 Brecht lived in Scandinavia; from 1941 to 1947 in California; he is now working at the playhouse in Zürich.

The coming of Hitler deprived Brecht for fourteen years of a public that spoke his own language. He spent the years of exile writing play after play — with no theater to try them out in. Only two of these plays — *The Private Life of the Master Race* and *Galileo* — have been professionally produced in the United States. Few of them have been published. We believe, therefore, that the present volume, in which two of Brecht's most recent plays are printed for the first time in any language, may be an eye-opener. Those who know Brecht's earlier work will find that he has, after all, gone on growing. And we hope that some who know nothing of Brecht but are interested in reading or producing plays will also be favorably impressed.

E. B. and M. B.

CONTENTS

THE GOOD WOMAN OF SETZUAN

PROLOGUE

A street. It is evening. Wang, the water seller, introduces him-self to the audience.

WANG. I sell water here in the city of Setzuan. It's a difficult business. When water is scarce, I have to go a long way to find any. And when it is plentiful, I am without income. But in our province there is nothing unusual about poverty. It is generally said that only the gods can still help us. From a cattle buyer who moves around a good deal, I learn to my unutterable joy that some of the highest gods are on their way to our province and may be expected here in Setzuan too. Heaven is said to be very disturbed by all the complaints that have been going up. For three days I have been waiting here at the entrance of the town, especially toward evening, so that I may be the first to greet them. Later, I'd hardly have the opportunity to do so. The gods will be surrounded by impor-tant people. They'll be in constant demand. If only I recog-nize them! After all they needn't come together. Perhaps they'll come separately so as not to be so conspicuous. It can't be those people over there, they are coming from work. (*He looks at passing workers.*) Their shoulders are crushed from all the carrying they do. That fellow there can't possibly be a god either, he has ink on his fingers. At best he's an office worker at a cement factory. Even those gentlemen there (*two gentlemen pass*) don't seem like gods to me. They look like people who're always beating somebody, which gods don't need to do. But look at those three! They're quite a different matter. They're well fed, show no sign of having any occupation, and have dust on their shoes, which means they come from far away. They must be gods. Dispose of me, illustrious ones!

(*He throws himself down before them.*)

THE FIRST GOD (*pleased*). Have we been expected here?

WANG (*giving them a drink*). For a long time. But I was the only one who *knew* you were coming.

THE FIRST GOD. Well, we need somewhere to stay the night. Do you know a place?

WANG. *A* place? Countless places! The whole town is at your service, illustrious ones! What sort of a place do you wish?

(*The Gods look meaningfully at each other.*)

THE FIRST GOD. Take the nearest house, my son! Try the very nearest house first.

WANG. I'm a little afraid of making enemies of other mighty men if I favor one of them in particular. Few people can help us, you see, but almost everyone can hurt us.

THE FIRST GOD. Well then, we order you: take the nearest house!

WANG. That is Mr. Fo over there! Wait just one moment!

(*He runs to a house and knocks at the door. It is opened, but one can see that he is rejected. He returns, hesitantly.*)

WANG. That's annoying. Mr. Fo is not at home just now, and his servants don't dare do anything without orders from him, he's so very strict. He will certainly have a fit when he learns who they turned away, won't he?

THE GODS (*smiling*). He certainly will.

WANG. Well then, another moment! The house next door belongs to the widow Su. She'll be beside herself with joy.

(*He runs to the house but apparently is rejected there too.*)

WANG. I'll have to inquire over there. She says she has only one little tiny room and it isn't prepared. I can well understand she's ashamed because some corners of the house aren't so clean. That's what women are like, it's a disgrace. I'll go at once to Mr. Tscheng.

THE SECOND GOD. The little room will be enough. Tell her we're coming.

4

WANG. Even if it isn't clean? It may be swarming with spiders!

THE SECOND GOD. That doesn't matter. Where there are spiders, there aren't so many flies.

THE THIRD GOD. Never mind. (*Friendly, to Wang*) Go to Mr. Tscheng or some other place, my son. Spiders, after all, rather disgust me.

(*Wang knocks again somewhere and is admitted.*)

VOICE FROM THE HOUSE. Spare us your gods! We have other troubles!

WANG (*back with the Gods*). Mr. Tscheng is quite upset. He has the whole house full of relations and doesn't dare show his face, illustrious ones! Between ourselves I believe there are bad people among them whom he doesn't want you to see. He is too afraid of your judgment, that's the thing.

THE THIRD GOD. Are we so terrible, then?

WANG. Only with bad people, isn't that so? It's well known, isn't it, that the province Kwan has been afflicted with floods for decades?

THE SECOND GOD. Really? Why?

WANG. Well, because there's no religion there!

THE SECOND GOD. Nonsense. It's because they neglected the dam!

THE FIRST GOD. Sst! (*To Wang*) Are you still hoping, my son?

WANG. How can you ask such a thing? I only need to go one house farther along. From there on, there'll be plenty to choose from. Everyone's just itching to put you up. Accidental circumstances, you understand. I go!

(*He begins to leave and then, undecided, remains standing in the street.*)

THE SECOND GOD. What did I say?

THE THIRD GOD. Of course it may really be "accidental circumstances."

THE SECOND GOD. In Schun, in Kwan, and in Setzuan —"accidental circumstances" every time? There aren't any religious people left, that's the naked truth, and you don't want to face it. Our mission has failed, why not admit it?

THE FIRST GOD. We might run across some good people at any moment. We mustn't expect things to be too cozy.

THE THIRD GOD. The resolution said: "The world can remain as it is if enough people are found living lives worthy of human beings." Good people, in other words. The water seller himself is such a person unless I'm very much mistaken. (*He goes up to Wang who is still standing undecided.*)

THE SECOND GOD. He *is* very much mistaken. When this water man gave us a drink from his measuring cup, I noticed something. Here's the cup. (*He shows it to the First God.*)

THE FIRST GOD. It has two bottoms.

THE SECOND GOD. A swindler!

THE FIRST GOD. All right, count *him* out. But what does it matter if *one* person is rotten? We'll find enough yet who'll meet our conditions. We have to find *one*! For two thousand years, they've been shouting: "The world can't go on as it is, no one on earth can *be* good and *stay* good." And now at last we've got to name the people who can keep our commandments.

THE THIRD GOD (*to Wang*). Is it so difficult to find a place?

WANG. Not for you! What are you thinking of? It's all my fault a place wasn't found right away. I'm not going about it properly.

THE THIRD GOD. Surely, that's not so.
(*He goes back.*)

WANG. They're noticing already. (*He accosts a gentlemen.*) Pardon me, worthy sir, for accosting you, but three of the highest gods, whose imminent arrival has been discussed for years by all Setzuan, have now actually appeared. They need a place to sleep. Do not pass by! See for yourself. One look will suffice. Don't wait, for heaven's sake. It's a chance in a lifetime! Be the first to ask the gods under your roof before they're snapped up by someone else. They will accept.
(*The gentleman has passed by.*)

WANG (*turning to another*). My dear sir, you've heard what's going on. Do you, perhaps, have spare rooms? They don't have to be palatial. It's the good intention that counts.

THE MAN. How should I know what kind of gods you've got there? A fellow that lets people into his house likes to know what he's getting.

6

(*He goes into a tobacco store. Wang runs back to the Three Gods.*)

WANG. I've found a gentleman who'll certainly take you.

(*He sees his cup on the ground, looks toward the Gods in confusion, takes it, and runs back again.*)

THE FIRST GOD. That doesn't sound encouraging.

WANG (*as the Man is coming out of the store again*). Well, what about the rooms for the night?

THE MAN. How do you know I don't live at an inn?

THE FIRST GOD. He's getting nowhere. We can cross Setzuan off the list too.

WANG. They're three of the very greatest gods! Really. Their statues in the temples are very well done. If you go quickly and invite them, they might accept!

THE MAN (*laughing*). You must be trying to find a place for a nice bunch of crooks. (*Exit.*)

WANG (*abusing him*). You squinting scoundrel! Have you no religion? You'll all roast in boiling oil for your indifference! The gods spit on you! But you'll regret it! You'll have to pay. The whole pack of you, fourth cousins included. You've brought disgrace to all Setzuan. (*pause*) And now only Shen Te the prostitute is left. She can't say no.

(*He calls* "Shen Te!" *Above, Shen Te looks out of the window.*)

WANG. They're here. I can't find any place to put them. Can't you take them in for the night?

SHEN TE. I don't think so, Wang. I'm expecting a gentleman. How is it you can't find any other place?

WANG. I can't tell you now. Setzuan is one big dung heap.

SHEN TE. When he comes I'd have to hide. Then maybe he'd go away again. He's expecting to take me out.

WANG. In the meantime, couldn't we come up?

SHEN TE. Well, you don't have to shout. Can we be open with them?

WANG. No! They musn't find out about your profession. We'd better wait downstairs. You won't go out with the gentleman then?

7

SHEN TE. I'm not so well off. And if I don't pay my rent by to-morrow morning, I'll be thrown out.

WANG. This is no time for calculations.

SHEN TE. I'm not so sure. Stomachs rumble even on the emperor's birthday. But all right, I'll take them in. (*She can be seen putting out the light.*)

THE FIRST GOD. I think it's hopeless.

(*They step up to Wang.*)

WANG (*starting as he sees them standing behind him*). A place has been found. (*He wipes the sweat off.*)

THE GODS. It has? Let's see it then.

WANG. There's no hurry. Take your time. The room still has to be fixed.

THE THIRD GOD. Well then, we'll sit down here and wait.

WANG. I'm afraid there's too much traffic right here. Perhaps we should go over there?

THE SECOND GOD. We like to look at people. That's what we're here for.

WANG. But . . . there's a draft.

THE SECOND GOD. Oh, we're pretty tough.

WANG. Perhaps you'd like me to show you Setzuan by night? We might take a little walk.

THE THIRD GOD. We've done quite a bit of walking today already. (*Smiling*) But if you want to get us away from here, you need only say so.

(*They go back.*)

THE THIRD GOD. Is this all right with you?

(*They sit down on a doorstep. Wang sits down on the ground at a little distance.*)

WANG (*taking a deep breath*). You're staying with a single girl. She's the best woman — the best human being — in Setzuan.

THE THIRD GOD. That's nice.

WANG (*to the audience*). When I picked up the cup a little while ago, they looked at me so strangely. Did they notice something? I don't dare look them in the eyes any more.

THE THIRD GOD. You're quite exhausted.

WANG. A little. From running.

THE FIRST GOD. Do people have a hard time of it here?

WANG. *Good* people do.

THE FIRST GOD (*seriously*). And you?

WANG. I know what you mean. I'm not good. But I don't have an easy time either.

(*In the meantime a gentleman has turned up in front of Shen Te's house. He has whistled several times. Each time Wang starts.*)

THE THIRD GOD (*softly, to Wang*). I think he's gone now.

WANG (*confused*). Yes.

(*He gets up and runs to the square, leaving his carrying pole behind. But in the meantime the waiting man has left, and Shen Te has stepped through the door and, softly calling "Wang!," has gone down the street. Wang, now softly calling "Shen Te!," gets no reply.*)

WANG. She's left me in the lurch. She's gone off to get her rent together and now I've no place for the illustrious ones. They're tired and still waiting. I can't go back again and say nothing doing. My own little place, a sewer pipe, is out of the question. Moreover, the gods wouldn't want to stay with a fellow when they've seen through his dishonest dealings. I won't go back. Not for anything in the world. But my carrying pole is lying there. What'll I do? I don't dare to get it. Since I didn't succeed in doing anything for the gods, whom I revere, I'll leave Setzuan and hide from their sight.

(*He rushes off. Shen Te returns. She is looking for Wang on the other side and sees the Gods.*)

SHEN TE. Are you the illustrious ones? My name is Shen Te. It would please me very much if you'd be content with my simple room.

THE THIRD GOD. Where has the water seller gone to?

SHEN TE. I must have missed him.

THE FIRST GOD. He probably thought you weren't coming and didn't dare return to us.

THE THIRD GOD (*picking up the carrying pole*). We'll leave this at your house. He'll be needing it.

(*Led by Shen Te, they go into the house. It grows dark, then*

9

light again. It is dawn. Again led by Shen Te, who lights their way with a lamp, the Gods pass through the door. They are taking leave.)

THE FIRST GOD. My dear Shen Te, we must thank you for your hospitality. We shall not forget that it was you who took us in. Return the carrying pole to the water seller and tell him that we want to thank him too for showing us a good human being.

SHEN TE. I'm not good. I have to confess something: when Wang asked me to put you up I hesitated.

THE FIRST GOD. Hesitating doesn't matter if only you win out. You must know that you did more than give us a place to sleep. Many — even some of us gods — have been doubting whether good people still exist. To decide that question is the main object of our journey. Now that we've found a good human being, we shall joyously continue on our way. Goodbye!

SHEN TE. Stop, illustrious ones! I'm not at all sure that I'm good. I'd like to be good of course, but how am I to pay my rent? Well, I'll confess it to you: I sell myself in order to live, and even so I can't get along. There are many others who have to do the same. I'm ready to do anything; but who isn't? I'd be happy to honor my father and my mother and speak the truth. It would be nice not to covet my neighbor's house. It would be pleasant to attach myself to one man and be faithful to him. I too should like not to exploit anyone, not to rob the helpless. But how? How? Even when I break only a *few* of the commandments, I can hardly survive.

THE FIRST GOD. All these, Shen Te, are but the doubts of a good woman.

THE THIRD GOD. Farewell, Shen Te! And give my best regards to the water seller. He was a good friend to us.

THE SECOND GOD. I fear he's none the better for it.

THE THIRD GOD. Best of luck to you!

THE FIRST GOD. Above all, be good, Shen Te! Farewell!

(*They turn to go. They are already waving.*)

SHEN TE (*worried*). But I'm not sure of myself, illustrious ones! How can I be good when everything is so expensive?

10

THE SECOND GOD. We can't do anything about that. We mustn't meddle with economics!

THE THIRD GOD. Stop! Just one moment! Might she not fare better if she were a little richer?

THE SECOND GOD. We can't give her anything. We couldn't account for it up above.

THE FIRST GOD. Why not?

(*They put their heads together and talk excitedly.*)

THE FIRST GOD (*embarrassed, to Shen Te*). You say you can't pay your rent. We're not paupers and of course we'll pay for the room. Here! (*He gives her money.*) But don't tell anyone we paid. Such an action could be misinterpreted.

THE SECOND GOD. It certainly could.

THE FIRST GOD. But it's allowable. We *can* pay for the room without misgiving. There's nothing against it in the resolution. Well, goodbye!

(*The Gods quickly go.*)

1

A small tobacco store. The store is not as yet completely furnished and has not opened.

SHEN TE (*to the audience*). It's now three days since the gods went away. They said they wanted to pay me for the night's lodging. And when I looked to see what they'd given me, I saw that it was more than a thousand silver dollars. With the money I bought myself a tobacco store. Yesterday I moved in here and I hope now to be able to do a lot of good. There, for instance, is Mrs. Shin, the former owner of the store. Yesterday she came to ask for rice for her children. Today I see her again coming across the square with her pot.

(*Enter Mrs. Shin. The two women bow to each other.*)

SHEN TE. Good morning, Mrs. Shin.

MRS. SHIN. Good morning, Miss Shen Te. How do you like it in your new home?

SHEN TE. Very much. How did your children spend the night?

MRS. SHIN. Oh dear, in a strange house, if you can call that shack a house! The youngest is coughing already.

SHEN TE. That's bad.

MRS. SHIN. You don't know what's bad. You're well off. But you'll learn quite a lot in this dump. What a slum this neighborhood is!

SHEN TE. Didn't you tell me the workers from the cement factory come here at noon?

MRS. SHIN. Yes, but otherwise there isn't a soul that buys here, not even the neighbors.

SHEN TE. You didn't tell me that when you sold me the store.

MRS. SHIN. Don't start blaming me now! First you rob me and my children of our home and then you call it a dump! And a slum! That's the limit! (*She cries.*)

SHEN TE (*quickly*). I'll get your rice right away.

MRS. SHIN. I also wanted to ask you to lend me some money.

SHEN TE (*pouring rice into Mrs. Shin's pot*). I can't. You know I haven't sold anything.

MRS. SHIN. But I need it. What am I to live off? You took everything away from me and now you cut my throat! I'll leave my children on your doorstep, you cutthroat! (*She tears the pot out of Shen Te's hands.*)

SHEN TE. Don't be angry! You'll spill the rice!

(*Enter an elderly couple and a shabbily dressed young man.*)

THE WIFE. Ah, my dear Shen Te, we've heard you're so well off now. You've become a businesswoman! Imagine, we're without a roof over our heads. Our tobacco store has gone to pieces. We were wondering whether we couldn't spend the night with you. You know my nephew? He's come too. He never leaves us.

THE NEPHEW (*looking around*). A nice store!

MRS. SHIN. What sort of people are *they*?

SHEN TE. They put me up when I first came in from the country. (*To the audience*) When the little money I had was gone, they threw me out on the street. Perhaps they're afraid now that I'll say no.

> They are poor.
> They have no shelter
> They have no friends
> They need somebody
> How could one say no?

(*Friendly, to the newcomers*) Welcome! I'll gladly give you shelter. Though I only have one very small room behind the store.

THE HUSBAND. That'll be enough. Don't worry.

THE WIFE (*while she brings tea to Shen Te*). We better settle down back here, so we won't be in your way. I suppose you've chosen a tobacco store in memory of your first home. We'll be able to give you some hints. That's another reason why we came.

MRS. SHIN (*sneering*). I hope customers will come too!

THE WIFE. I guess that's meant for us.

THE HUSBAND. Psst! Here comes a customer.

(*A ragged man comes in.*)

THE RAGGED MAN. Excuse me. I am unemployed.

(*Mrs. Shin laughs.*)

SHEN TE. Can I help you?

THE UNEMPLOYED. I hear you're opening up tomorrow. Things sometimes get damaged when you're unpacking. Don't you have a spare cigarette?

THE WIFE. What nerve, begging for tobacco! He might at least ask for bread!

THE UNEMPLOYED. Bread is expensive. A few puffs at a cigarette and I'll be a new man. I'm all in.

SHEN TE (*giving him cigarettes*). That's important, to be a new man. I'll open the store with you as my first customer. You'll bring me luck.

(*The Unemployed quickly lights a cigarette, inhales, and goes off, coughing.*)

THE WIFE. My dear Shen Te, was that right?

MRS. SHIN. If you open up like this, in three days there'll be no store left.

THE HUSBAND. I bet he still had money in his pocket.

SHEN TE. But he said he hadn't.

THE NEPHEW. How do you know he wasn't lying?

SHEN TE (*angrily*). How do I know he *was* lying?

THE WIFE (*shaking her head*). She can't say no! You're too good, Shen Te. If you want to keep your store, you must learn to say no, now and then.

THE HUSBAND. Why don't you say it's not yours? Say it belongs to a relative who insists on an exact settlement of accounts. Can't you do that?

MRS. SHIN. That could be done if one wasn't always pretending to be a benefactress.

SHEN TE (*laughing*). Scold, scold, scold! If you're not careful I'll give you notice and pour the rice back.

THE WIFE (*horrified*). The rice is yours, too?

SHEN TE (*to the audience*).

> They are bad.
> They are nobody's friend.
> They begrudge everyone his rice.
> They need everything themselves.
> Who could scold them?

(*Enter a little man.*)

MRS. SHIN (*seeing him and hurriedly starting to go*). I'll see you tomorrow. (*Exit.*)

THE LITTLE MAN (*calling after her*). Stop, Mrs. Shin! It's you I'm looking for.

THE WIFE. Does she come regularly? Does she have any claim on you?

SHEN TE. She has no claim, but she's hungry: that's more than a claim.

THE LITTLE MAN. *She* knows why she's running. You're the new owner? Oh, you're filling up the shelves already. But

14

they don't belong to you, see! Unless you pay for them. The rascals who were here before didn't pay for them. (*To the others*) I'm the carpenter, you see.

SHEN TE. But I thought they belonged to the furnishings, which I paid for.

THE CARPENTER. Fraud! It's all a fraud! You're working together with that Shin woman of course. I demand my hundred silver dollars as sure as my name's Lin To.

SHEN TE. How am I to pay it? I have no more money!

THE CARPENTER. Then I'll have you arrested. You'll pay at once or I'll have you arrested.

THE HUSBAND (*prompting Shen Te*). Cousin!

SHEN TE. Can't it wait till next month?

THE CARPENTER (*shouting*). No!

SHEN TE. Don't be hard, Mr. Lin To. I can't settle all claims at once. (*To the audience*)

> A little indulgence and strength is redoubled.
> Look, the cart horse stops and sniffs the grass:
> Connive at this and the horse will pull better.
> A little patience in June and the tree is heavy
>   with peaches in August.
> How should we live together without patience?
> A short postponement, and the farthest goals are
>   reached.

(*To the Carpenter*) Be patient just for a little while, Mr. Lin To!

THE CARPENTER. And who's patient with me and my family? (*He moves a shelf from the wall as if he wanted to take it with him.*) Pay up, or I take the shelves away!

THE WIFE. My dear Shen Te, why don't you let your cousin settle this affair? (*To the Carpenter*) Write down your claim and Miss Shen Te's cousin will pay.

THE CARPENTER. Cousin! I know these cousins!

THE NEPHEW. Don't laugh like that! I know him personally.

THE HUSBAND. What a man! Sharp as a knife!

THE CARPENTER. All right, he'll get my bill! (*He puts down a shelf, sits on it, and writes out his bill.*)

15

THE WIFE (*to Shen Te*). If you don't stop him, he'll tear the shirt off your body to get his measly shelves. Never recognize a claim, justified or not, or in two minutes you'll be swamped with claims, justified or not. Throw a piece of meat into a garbage can, and all the mangy dogs of the district will be at each other's throats in your back yard. What are our law courts for?

SHEN TE. If his work doesn't support him, the law courts won't. He's done some work and doesn't want to go empty-handed. And he's got a family. It's too bad I can't pay him. What will the gods say?

THE HUSBAND. You did your share when you took *us* in. That's more than enough.

(*Enter a limping man and a pregnant woman.*)

THE LIMPING MAN (*to the couple*). Oh, here you are! You're nice relatives! Leaving us standing on the street corner.

THE WIFE (*embarrassed, to Shen Te*). That's my brother Wung and my sister-in-law. (*To the two of them*) Stop grumbling. Go and sit quietly in the corner and don't disturb our old friend, Miss Shen Te. You can stay here, she's got nothing against it. (*To Shen Te*) I think we've got to take these two in. My sister-in-law is in her fifth month. Or don't you agree?

SHEN TE. Oh, yes. Welcome!

THE WIFE. (*to the two*). Say thank you. The cups are back there. (*To Shen Te*) They just wouldn't have known *where* to go. A good thing you got the store!

SHEN TE (*laughing, and bringing tea, she says to the audience*). Yes, a good thing I did!

(*Enter the Landlady, Mrs. Mi Tzu, a blank in her hand.*)

THE LANDLADY. Miss Shen Te, I am the landlady, Mrs. Mi Tzu. I hope we'll get on well together. Here is the lease. (*While Shen Te is reading through the lease*) The opening of a little store is a beautiful moment, isn't it, ladies and gentlemen? (*She looks around.*) There're still a few small gaps on the shelves, but it'll be all right. You'll be able to bring me some references, won't you?

SHEN TE. Is that necessary?

16

THE LANDLADY. I've no idea who you are.

THE HUSBAND. Perhaps we can vouch for Miss Shen Te? We've known her since she came to town and will go through fire for her at any time.

THE LANDLADY. And who are you?

THE HUSBAND. I am the tobacco dealer Ma Fu.

THE LANDLADY. Where's your store?

THE HUSBAND. At the moment I don't have a store. I've just sold it.

THE LANDLADY. I see. (*To Shen Te*) And don't you know anyone else who could give me some information about you?

THE WIFE (*prompting*). Cousin! Cousin!

THE LANDLADY. You've got to have somebody to speak for you if you're coming into my house. This is a respectable house, my dear. Without some assurance I can't even sign the lease with you.

SHEN TE (*slowly, with downcast eyes*). I have a cousin.

THE LANDLADY. Oh, you have a cousin. On the square? Then we can go over there right away. What does he do?

SHEN TE. He isn't living here. He's in another town.

THE WIFE. Didn't you say he was in Shung?

SHEN TE. Mr. . . . Shui Ta. In Shung.

THE HUSBAND. But I know him! A tall thin fellow?

THE NEPHEW (*to the Carpenter*). *You* were negotiating with Miss Shen Te's cousin too! About the shelves!

THE CARPENTER (*surly*). I'm just writing out a bill for him. Here it is! (*He hands it over.*) Tomorrow morning I'll be back. (*Exit.*)

THE NEPHEW (*calling after him and glancing at the Landlady*). Don't worry, the cousin will pay!

THE LANDLADY (*examining Shen Te closely*). Well, I'll be very pleased to meet him too. Good evening, Miss. (*Exit.*)

THE WIFE (*after a pause*). Now the cat's out of the bag. You can be sure she'll know everything about you tomorrow morning.

THE SISTER-IN-LAW (*softly to the Nephew*). This thing won't last long!

17

(*Enter a boy leading an old man.*)

THE BOY (*calling over his shoulder*). Here they are.

THE WIFE. Good evening, Grandfather. (*To Shen Te*) The good old man! He must have worried about us. And the boy, hasn't he grown? He eats like ten men. Well, who else did you bring, for heaven's sake?

THE HUSBAND (*looking outside*). Only our niece.

THE SISTER-IN-LAW (*softly to the Nephew while a young girl comes in*). The rats climb onto the sinking ship!

THE WIFE (*to Shen Te*). A young relative from the country. I hope we aren't too many for you. We weren't quite as many when you were living with us, were we? Yes, we got more and more. The less we had, the more there were of us. And the more there were of us, the less we had. But now we'll lock up, or there won't be a moment's peace. (*She locks the door and they all sit down.*) We mustn't disturb you in your business, that's the main thing. Or how can the fire be kept burning? We thought we might arrange matters something like this: during the day the young ones will go off and only grandfather, the sister-in-law, and maybe I myself will stay. The others will look in at the most once or twice during the day, all right? Light the lamp over there and make yourself at home.

THE NEPHEW (*humorously*). If only the cousin doesn't pop up tonight all of a sudden. The strict Mr. Shui Ta!

(*The Sister-in-law laughs.*)

THE BROTHER (*reaching for a cigarette*). One cigarette won't matter much.

THE HUSBAND. I'm sure it won't.

(*They all help themselves to cigarettes. The Brother hands round a jug of wine.*)

THE NEPHEW. The cousin will pay for it.

THE GRANDFATHER (*seriously to Shen Te*). Good evening!

(*Shen Te is confused by the belated greeting and bows. In one hand she holds the Carpenter's bill, in the other the lease.*)

THE WIFE. Couldn't you sing something to entertain our hostess a little?

18

THE NEPHEW. Grandfather will start!
(*They sing.*)

THE SONG OF THE SMOKE

THE GRANDFATHER.

There was a time — before old age had bleached
my hair —
I hoped I might survive by being clever.
But when does cleverness alone suffice
To fill a poor man's belly? Never, never!
That's why I said: let go!
Watch the grey smoke float
Ever into colder coldness: so
Sails your boat.

THE HUSBAND.

I saw the honest, conscientious man oppressed
So by the crooked path I tried to go.
But that path also leads us only downward
And what to do I don't pretend to know.
And so I say: let go!
Watch the grey smoke float
Ever into colder coldness: so
Sails your boat.

THE NIECE.

The old, I hear, have nothing left to hope for.
Since only time can heal, they're in a fix.
But for the young, I hear, the door is open.
It opens, so they tell me, upon nix.
So I too say: let go!
Watch the grey smoke float
Ever into colder coldness: so
Sails your boat.

THE NEPHEW. Where did you get the wine?
THE SISTER-IN-LAW. He pawned the bag of tobacco.
THE HUSBAND. What? That tobacco was the only thing left to us!
We didn't even touch it to pay for our lodgings! You swine!
THE BROTHER. Do you call me a swine because my wife is cold?

19

And you had a drink yourself? Give me the jug this minute! (*They fight. The shelves fall over.*)

SHEN TE (*imploring them*). Oh, spare the store! Don't destroy everything! It's a gift of the gods! Take what there is, but don't destroy it all!

THE WIFE (*skeptically*). The store is smaller than I thought. Perhaps we shouldn't have mentioned it to Auntie and the others. If they come too, it'll be very crowded.

THE SISTER-IN-LAW. Our hostess is cooling off already.

(*There are voices outside and a knocking on the door.*)

SHOUTS FROM OUTSIDE. Open up! It's us!

THE WIFE. Is that you, Auntie? What are we going to do?

SHEN TE. O hope! My beautiful store! I bought it yesterday and today it's done for.

> The little lifeboat
> Is swiftly sent down
> Too many people greedily
> Reach for it as they drown.

SHOUTS FROM OUTSIDE. Open up!

1·A

Below a bridge. The water seller crouches by the river.

WANG (*looking around*). Everything's quiet. It's four days now that I've been hiding out. They can't find me, because I'm keeping my eyes open. I fled along their road on purpose. On the second day, they passed the bridge, I heard their steps above me. Now they must be a long way off, and I'm safe. (*He lies back and falls asleep. Music. The slope becomes transparent and the Gods appear.*)

WANG (*raising his arm to his face as if about to be struck*). Don't say anything! I know it all! I found no one who wants to take you, not in a single house! Now you know! Now you can go on!

THE FIRST GOD. But you did find someone. When you were away, she came. She took us in for the night, she watched over our sleep, and when we left her in the morning she showed us the way with a lamp. You mentioned her to us as a good woman and she was good.

WANG. So it was Shen Te who took you in?

THE THIRD GOD. Of course.

WANG. And I had so little faith, I ran away! Only because I thought: "She can't come. Because she's not well off, she can't come."

THE GODS.

O weak one!

O well-disposed but weak man!

Where there is need, he thinks, there is no goodness!

Where there is danger, he thinks, there is no courage!

O weakness always to believe the worst!

O hasty judgment! Frivolous despair!

WANG. I'm very ashamed, illustrious ones!

THE FIRST GOD. And now, water seller, do us a favor and go back quickly to the city of Setzuan. Look up the good Shen Te there and give us a report on her. She's well off now. She's supposed to have got some money for a little store so she can follow the inclinations of her heart. Show an interest in her goodness. No one can be good for long when goodness is not in demand. We will continue our journey. We will search and find other people who resemble our good woman from Setzuan: the talk about good people being no longer able to live on our earth will stop. (*They disappear.*)

2

The tobacco store. People sleeping everywhere. The lamp is still burning. A knocking.

THE WIFE (*getting up, sleepily*). Shen Te! Someone's knocking! Where is she, anyway?

THE NEPHEW. I guess she's getting breakfast. The cousin will pay for it!
(*The Wife laughs and shuffles to the door. Enter a young man, followed by the Carpenter.*)

THE YOUNG MAN. I'm the cousin.

THE WIFE (*falling from the clouds*). What?!

THE YOUNG MAN. My name is Shui Ta.

THE GUESTS (*shaking each other awake*). Her cousin! But that was a joke, she doesn't *have* a cousin! Someone's here saying he's her cousin! I don't believe it, so early in the morning!

THE NEPHEW. If you're our hostess's cousin, go and get us some breakfast quickly!

SHUI TA (*putting out the light*). The first customers will soon be here. Please get dressed so that I can open my store.

THE HUSBAND. *Your* store? I thought the store belonged to our friend Shen Te. (*Shui Ta shakes his head.*) What, it isn't her store at all?

THE SISTER-IN-LAW. Then she's cheated us! Where is she, anyway?

SHUI TA. She's been delayed. She wants me to tell you that, now *I'm* here, she can no longer do anything for you.

THE WIFE (*deeply affected*). And we thought she was good!

THE NEPHEW. Don't believe him! Look for her!

THE HUSBAND. That's what we'll do. (*He organizes the search.*) You and you and you and you, look for her everywhere. Grandfather and us, we'll stay here to hold the fort. In the meantime the boy can get us something to eat. (*To the Boy*) You see the bakery over there on the corner? Sneak over and stuff your shirt full.

THE SISTER-IN-LAW. Take a few of the little light cakes too!

THE HUSBAND. But be careful, don't let the baker catch you! And don't run into the policeman!

(*The Boy nods and goes off. The others finish dressing.*)

SHUI TA. This store has been your refuge. Won't you give it a bad reputation if you steal from the bakery?

THE NEPHEW. Don't pay any attention to him. We'll find her soon enough. She'll give him a piece of her mind.

(*The Nephew, the Brother, the Sister-in-law, and the Niece go out.*)

THE SISTER-IN-LAW (*as she leaves*). Leave us some of the breakfast!

SHUI TA (*calmly*). You won't find her. My cousin regrets of course that she can't abide by the law of hospitality for an unlimited period. But unfortunately there are too many of you. This is a tobacco store and Miss Shen Te has to live off it.

THE HUSBAND. Our Shen Te just couldn't say a thing like that.

SHUI TA. Perhaps you're right. (*To the Carpenter*) The unfortunate thing is that the need in this city is too great for a single person to manage. In that regard, nothing has changed, unfortunately, since someone eleven hundred years ago composed these lines:

The governor, asked what was needed
To help the freezing people of the town, made answer:
"A blanket ten thousand feet long
Which would simply cover all the suburbs."

(*He starts to clean up the store.*)

THE CARPENTER. I see you're trying to put your cousin's affairs in order. There's a little debt, recognized by witnesses, and it needs settling. For the shelves. One hundred silver dollars.

SHUI TA (*taking the bill out of his pocket, not unfriendly*). Don't you think one hundred silver dollars a little much?

THE CARPENTER. No. And I can't make any deductions. I have a wife and children to support.

SHUI TA (*severely*). How many children?

THE CARPENTER. Four.

23

SHUI TA. Then I offer you twenty silver dollars.

(*The Husband laughs.*)

THE CARPENTER. Are you crazy? The shelves are walnut!

SHUI TA. Then take them away.

THE CARPENTER. What d'you mean?

SHUI TA. They cost too much. I beg you, take the walnut shelves away.

THE WIFE. Well said! (*She laughs too.*)

THE CARPENTER (*uncertainly*). I demand that someone call Miss Shen Te. She seems to be a better person than you.

SHUI TA. Certainly. She's ruined.

THE CARPENTER (*resolutely taking some shelves and carrying them to the door*). You can pile up your tobacco goods on the floor! It suits me!

SHUI TA (*to the Husband*). Help him!

THE HUSBAND (*he also grabs a shelf and, grinning, carries it to the door*). Out with the shelves!

THE CARPENTER. You dog, do you want my family to starve?

SHUI TA. Once more I offer you twenty silver dollars. I don't want to pile up my tobacco goods on the floor.

THE CARPENTER. A hundred!

(*Shui Ta looks indifferently out of the window. The Husband prepares to carry out more shelves.*)

THE CARPENTER. At least don't smash them against the door post, idiot! (*Desperately*) But they were made to measure! They fit this dump and nowhere else! The boards are spoiled, mister!

SHUI TA. Exactly. That's why I'm offering you only twenty silver dollars. Because the boards are spoiled.

(*The Wife squeals with pleasure.*)

THE CARPENTER (*suddenly tired*). I can't keep it up. Take the shelves and pay what you want.

SHUI TA. Twenty silver dollars.

(*He places two large coins on the table. The Carpenter takes them.*)

THE HUSBAND (*carrying back the shelves*). It's enough for a heap of spoiled boards!

THE CARPENTER. Enough, maybe, to get drunk on! (*Exit.*)

THE HUSBAND. We got rid of *him*!

THE WIFE (*weeping with merriment and drying her tears*). "They're walnut!" "Take them away!" "One hundred silver dollars! I have four children!" "Then I'll pay twenty!" "But they're spoiled." "Exactly! Twenty silver dollars!"— That's how one has to treat those scamps.

SHUI TA. Yes. (*Earnestly*) Go away quickly!

THE HUSBAND. Us?

SHUI TA. Yes, you. You're thieves and parasites. If you go fast without wasting time talking back, you can still save yourselves.

THE HUSBAND. It's best just not to answer him at all. Let's not shout on an empty stomach. I'd like to know where the boy is.

SHUI TA. Yes, where's the boy? I told you before, I don't want him in my store with stolen cakes. (*Suddenly shouting*) Once more: Go!

(*They remain seated.*)

SHUI TA (*calmly again*). As you wish.

(*He goes to the door and bows low. A Policeman appears in the doorway.*)

SHUI TA. I presume I am addressing the officer in charge of this neighborhood?

THE POLICEMAN. Yes, Mr. . . .

SHUI TA. Shui Ta. (*They smile at each other.*) Nice weather today!

THE POLICEMAN. A little warm, maybe?

SHUI TA. A little warm, maybe.

THE HUSBAND (*softly to the Wife*). If he gabbles until the boy comes back, we're done for!

(*He tries secretly to make some signs at Shui Ta.*)

SHUI TA (*without paying attention to him*). It makes a difference whether one thinks of the weather from a cool store or from the dusty street.

THE POLICEMAN. A big difference.

THE WIFE (*to the Husband*). Don't worry! The boy won't come when he sees the policeman standing in the doorway.

25

SHUI TA. Why don't you come in? It's really cooler in here. My cousin and I have opened a store. We attach the greatest importance, let me tell you, to being on good terms with the authorities.

THE POLICEMAN (*entering*). You are very kind, Mr. Shui Ta. Yes, it's really cool in here.

THE HUSBAND (*softly*). He's taking him in, specially so the boy won't see him.

SHUI TA. Visitors. Distant acquaintances of my cousin, I hear. They are on a journey. (*They bow.*) We were just about to take leave.

THE HUSBAND (*hoarsely*). Well, we'll be going now.

SHUI TA. I shall tell my cousin that you want to thank her for the rooms but that you had no time to await her return.

(*A noise from the street and shouts of*: "Stop thief!")

THE POLICEMAN. What's that?

(*The Boy is in the doorway. Various kinds of cakes are falling out of his shirt. The Wife waves him desperately back. He turns and starts to go.*)

THE POLICEMAN. Stop, you! (*He takes hold of the Boy.*) Where did you get these cakes?

THE BOY. Over there.

THE POLICEMAN. Oh, theft, is it?

THE WIFE. We didn't know anything about it. The boy did it on his own. (*To the Boy*) You good-for-nothing!

THE POLICEMAN. Mr. Shui Ta, can you clarify the situation? (*Shui Ta is silent.*)

THE POLICEMAN. Aha. You're all coming to the station with me.

SHUI TA. I'm most distressed that such a thing could have happened in my establishment.

THE WOMAN. He was watching when the boy went away!

SHUI TA. I can assure you, officer, I should hardly have asked you in if I'd wanted to conceal a theft.

THE POLICEMAN. That's right. And you will also understand, Mr. Shui Ta, that it's my duty to take those people away. (*Shui Ta bows.*) Go on with you! (*He drives them out.*)

THE GRANDFATHER (*solemnly from the doorway*). Good day!

(*Exeunt all except Shui Ta, who continues to tidy up. Enter the Landlady.*)

THE LANDLADY. So you're her cousin! What does it mean that the police are dragging people away from my house? What right has your Miss Shen Te to turn this store into a house of assignation? That's what happens if one takes in people who only yesterday lived in a two-bit hotel and went begging for bread to the corner bakery! You see, I know everything!

SHUI TA. Yes, I see. You've been told bad things about my cousin. She is accused of having gone hungry! It's a notorious fact that she lived in poverty. She's got the worst possible reputation: that of being poor.

THE LANDLADY. She was a common . . .

SHUI TA. Pauper. Let's not mince words.

THE LANDLADY. Oh, please, no sentimental rubbish. I'm speaking about her conduct, not her earnings. There must have been earnings, or this store wouldn't be here. Several elderly gentlemen must have taken care of that. How does one get a store at all? Sir, this is a respectable house! The people who pay rent here don't wish to live under the same roof with such a person. Yes, sir. (*pause*) I'm not a monster but I've got to be careful.

SHUI TA (*coldly*). Mrs. Mi Tzu, I'm busy. Just tell me how much it'll cost us to live in this respectable house.

THE LANDLADY. You're a cool customer, I must say.

SHUI TA (*taking the lease from the counter*). The rent is very high. I assume from the contract that it's payable by the month.

THE LANDLADY (*quickly*). Not for people like your cousin!

SHUI TA. What do you mean?

THE LANDLADY. I mean that people like your cousin must pay the half-yearly rent of two hundred silver dollars in advance.

SHUI TA. Two hundred silver dollars! Sheer usury! How am I to get it? I can't count on a large turnover here. My only hope lies in the sack makers at the cement factory. I've been told they smoke a lot because their work is exhausting. But then, *they* don't earn much either.

27

THE LANDLADY. You should have thought of that earlier.

SHUI TA. Mrs. Mi Tzu, have a heart! It's true, my cousin has made the unpardonable mistake of giving shelter to unfortunate persons. But she can improve. I'll see to it that she improves. And, tell me, how could you find a better tenant than one who knows the depths because she comes from them? She'll work her fingers to the bone to pay the rent on time. She'll do everything, sacrifice everything, sell everything, shun nothing, and all the time she'll be as humble as a little mouse and as quiet as a fly. She'll give way to you in anything before she'll go back where she came from. Such a tenant is worth her weight in gold.

THE LANDLADY. Two hundred silver dollars payable in advance or she'll go back on the streets where she came from!

(*Enter the Policeman.*)

THE POLICEMAN. Don't let me disturb you, Mr. Shui Ta!

THE LANDLADY. The police certainly display a great interest in this store.

THE POLICEMAN. Mrs. Mi Tzu, I hope you haven't got the wrong impression. Mr. Shui Ta has done us a service and I'm coming solely to thank him for it in the name of the police.

THE LANDLADY. Well, that's nothing to me. I hope, Mr. Shui Ta, that my proposal will be agreeable to your cousin. I like to be on good terms with my tenants. Good day, gentlemen. (*Exit.*)

SHUI TA. Good day, Mrs. Mi Tzu.

THE POLICEMAN. Are you having difficulties with Mrs. Mi Tzu.

SHUI TA. She's demanding the rent in advance because my cousin doesn't seem to her respectable.

THE POLICEMAN. And you don't have the money? (*Shui Ta is silent.*) But surely a man like you, Mr. Shui Ta, can get credit?

SHUI TA. Perhaps. But how can a woman like Shen Te get credit?

THE POLICEMAN. Aren't you staying?

SHUI TA. No. I can't come back either. I can lend her a helping hand only on my trip through town. I can only ward off the worst. Soon she'll have to rely on herself again. I'm wondering what will happen then? I'm worried.

THE POLICEMAN. Mr. Shui Ta, I'm sorry you're in difficulties with the rent. I must admit that at first we looked at this store with mixed feelings. But your courageous behavior a little while ago showed us what you're made of. The authorities soon find out who they can trust.

SHUI TA (*bitterly*). Officer, in order to save this little store, which my cousin regards as a gift of the gods, I'm ready to go to the very limit permitted by law. But hardness and cunning help only against inferiors. The lines are drawn cleverly. I feel like the man who dealt with the rats, only to find himself with rivers to cross. (*After a little pause*) Do you smoke?

THE POLICEMAN (*putting two cigars into his pocket*). Us fellows at the station would hate to lose you, Mr. Shui Ta. But you've got to understand Mrs. Mi Tzu. Shen Te — let's not beat about the bush — lived by selling herself to men. You can object: what else could she have done? How, for instance, was she to pay her rent? But the fact remains: it isn't respectable. Why not? First: one doesn't sell love — beware of the love that's for sale! Second: it's respectable to go with someone you love but not with someone who's paying for it! Third: the proverb says, not for a handful of rice but for love! Well, you'll answer, what good is all this wisdom once the milk is spilt? What can she do? She's got to get hold of her half-year's rent or she'll be back on the streets. And how's she to get hold of the rent? Mr. Shui Ta, I have to tell you, I don't know. (*He's busy thinking.*) Mr. Shui Ta, I've got it! Find her a husband!

(*Enter a little old woman.*)

THE OLD WOMAN. A good cheap cigar for my husband. We'll have been married forty years tomorrow, you see, and we're having a little celebration.

SHUI TA (*politely*). Forty years, and you still want to celebrate!

THE OLD WOMAN. As far as our means allow! We own the carpet store across from here. I hope we'll be good neighbors. We should be. Times are bad.

29

SHUI TA (*showing her various boxes*). A very old saying, I fear.

THE POLICEMAN. Mr. Shui Ta, we need capital. Well, I propose a marriage.

SHUI TA (*apologetically to the Old Woman*). I've let myself be persuaded to bother this gentleman with my personal worries.

THE POLICEMAN. We can't pay the half-year's rent. Very well. We marry a little money.

SHUI TA. That won't be easy.

THE POLICEMAN. Why not? She's a good match. She's got a small, growing store. (*To the Old Woman*) What do *you* thing about it?

THE OLD WOMAN (*undecidedly*). Yes . . .

THE POLICEMAN. An ad in the paper!

THE OLD WOMAN (*reticently*). If the young lady agrees . . .

THE POLICEMAN. What should she have against it? I'll make out the ad. One good turn deserves another. Don't think the authorities aren't concerned with the struggling small businessman! You lend us a helping hand and in return we make up a matrimonial ad for you! Ha! ha! ha!
(*He eagerly takes out his notebook, wets the stump of a pencil, and writes away.*)

SHUI TA (*slowly*). It's not a bad idea.

THE POLICEMAN. "What . . . decent . . . man with small capital . . . widower . . . not excluded . . . wishes . . . marriage . . . into flourishing tobacco store?" And then we'll add: "am . . . pretty . . . pleasant appearance." How's that?

SHUI TA. If you don't think that's an exaggeration . . .

THE OLD WOMAN (*kindly*). Not at all. I've seen her.
(*The Policeman tears the page out of his notebook and hands it to Shui Ta.*)

SHUI TA. With horror I see how much luck one needs to keep above water. How many ideas! How many friends! (*To the Policeman*) Despite my determination, I was at the end of my tether as far as the store rent was concerned. But then you came and helped me with good advice. Truly, now I see a way out!

30

3

*Evening in the city park. A young man — Yang Sun — in
ragged clothes follows with his eyes an airplane which seems
to be describing a curve high over the city park. He takes a
rope out of his pocket and looks carefully around. As he is
going toward a large willow, two prostitutes come along. The
one is already old, the other is the niece from the family that
has imposed itself on Shen Te.*

THE YOUNG ONE. Good evening, young gentleman. Coming with
me, dearie?

SUN. Perhaps, ladies. If you buy me something to eat.

THE OLD ONE. You're nuts, aren't you? (*To the Young One*)
Let's go on. We're only wasting our time with him. He's the
unemployed pilot.

THE YOUNG ONE. But no one else will be left in the park, it'll
rain in a minute.

THE OLD ONE. You never know.

(*They go on. Sun, looking about, pulls out his rope and
throws it round a willow branch. But again he is disturbed.
The two prostitutes are coming quickly back. They don't see
him.*)

THE YOUNG ONE. It's going to pour.

(*Shen Te comes walking along.*)

THE OLD ONE. Look, here comes the monster! She brought dis-
aster to you and your family!

THE YOUNG ONE. It wasn't her. It was her cousin. She took us
in and later offered to pay for the cakes. I have nothing
against her.

THE OLD ONE. But I have! (*loudly*) Ah, here's our dear rich
sister! She's got a store but she still wants to snatch our boy
friends away.

SHEN TE. Now don't bite my head off. I'm going to the tearoom
by the pond.

THE YOUNG ONE. Is it true you're going to marry a widower
with three children?

SHEN TE. Yes, I'm meeting him there.

SUN (*impatiently*). Won't you get going, you whores! Can't a man be at peace even here?

THE OLD ONE. Shut your trap!

(*Exeunt the two prostitutes.*)

SUN (*calling after them*). Vultures! (*To the audience*) Even at this remote spot they don't tire of fishing for victims! Even in the bushes, even when it's raining, they desperately search for customers!

SHEN TE (*angrily*). Why do you swear at them? (*She notices the rope.*) Oh!

SUN. What are you gaping at?

SHEN TE. What's the rope for?

SUN. Go on, sister, go on! I've no money, nothing, not even a penny. And if I had a penny, I wouldn't buy you. First I'd buy a cup of water.

(*It starts raining.*)

SHEN TE. What's the rope for? You mustn't do that!

SUN. What's that to you? Clear off!

SHEN TE. It's raining.

SUN. Don't you try to come under this tree.

SHEN TE (*who stays standing in the rain without moving*). No.

SUN. Sister, leave it, it won't help you. You can't do business with me. You're too ugly for me anyway. Crooked legs.

SHEN TE. That isn't true.

SUN. Don't show them! If it's raining, for heaven's sake come under the tree!

(*She goes slowly under the tree and sits down.*)

SHEN TE. Why did you want to do it?

SUN. Do you want to know? Then I'll tell you: to get rid of you. (*pause*) Do you know what it is to be a flier?

SHEN TE. Yes, I've seen pilots in a tearoom.

SUN. No, you haven't. Perhaps you've seen a couple of conceited idiots with leather helmets, fellows with no ear for a motor, no sense for a machine. They only get into a plane because they know how to bribe the manager at the airport. Tell one of them: "Take your plane two thousand feet up, let it fall down through the clouds, and then catch it with one flick of the wrist," and he'll say: "That's not in the contract." If you fly, and you don't land your plane as if you were landing on your own rear end, you are not a flier but a fool. I am a flier. And I'm also the biggest fool for reading all those books on flying in the school at Peking and missing out on one page of one book which says that there's no need for fliers any more. And so I'm a flier without a plane, a mail pilot without mail. *You* can't understand what that means.

SHEN TE. I think I can.

SUN. No, I'm telling you, you can't understand it. That means you can't understand it.

SHEN TE (*half laughing, half crying*). When we were children we had a crane with a lame wing. He was friendly and didn't mind our jokes. He strutted along behind us, crying out to us not to run too fast. But in the fall and in the spring when large swarms of cranes were flying over the village, he became very restless. And I could understand why. (*She weeps.*)

SUN. Don't howl.

SHEN TE. No.

SUN. It hurts the complexion.

SHEN TE. I'm stopping.

(*She dries her tears with her sleeve. Leaning against the tree, and without turning toward her, he reaches for her face.*)

SUN. You don't even know how to wipe your face properly.

(*He wipes it for her with a handkerchief. Pause.*)

SUN. If you *had* to stay here so I wouldn't hang myself, you might at least open your mouth.

SHEN TE. I don't know anything.

SUN. Why exactly do you want to cut me down from the tree, sister?

SHEN TE. I'm frightened. I'm sure you only wanted to do it because the evening is so gloomy. (*To the audience*)

> In our country
> There should be no gloomy evenings.

33

High bridges over the river
The hour between night and morning
And the long winter: they too are dangerous.
For with all the misery
A little is enough
And men throw away
The unbearable life.

SUN. Talk about yourself.

SHEN TE. What about me? I have a little store.

SUN (*mocking*). Oh, you don't walk the streets, you have a
store!

SHEN TE (*determinedly*). I have a store now, but, before, I was
on the streets.

SUN. And the store was a gift of the gods, I suppose?

SHEN TE. Yes.

SUN. One nice evening they were standing there and saying:
Here's some money?

SHEN TE (*laughing softly*). One morning.

SUN. You're not exactly entertaining.

SHEN TE (*after a pause*). I can play the zither a little, and I
can mimic people. (*In a low voice she imitates a man of
dignity.*) "Well, think of that, I must have left my money at
home!" But then I got the store. And the first thing I did was
to give away my zither. Now, I said to myself, I can be as
dumb as a fish and it won't make any difference.

> I'm rich now, I said.
> I walk alone, I sleep alone.
> For a whole year, I said,
> I'll have nothing to do with a man.

SUN. But now you're marrying one? The one in the tearoom by
the pond?

(*Shen Te is silent.*)

SUN. What exactly do you know of love?

SHEN TE. Everything.

SUN. Nothing, sister. (*pause*) Or perhaps you liked it?

SHEN TE. No.

34

SUN (*without turning toward her, he strokes her face with his hand*). Is that pleasant?

SHEN TE. Yes.

SUN. You're easily satisfied, I must say. What a town!

SHEN TE. Don't you have any friends?

SUN. Lots, but none who want to hear I'm still without a job. They make a face as if someone was complaining that there's still water in the ocean. Do *you* have a friend maybe?

SHEN TE (*hesitantly*). A cousin.

SUN. Then beware of him.

SHEN TE. He's only been here once. Now he's gone away and he'll never be back. But why are you talking so despairingly? To speak without hope, they say, is to speak without goodness.

SUN. Just go on talking. A voice, after all, is a voice.

SHEN TE (*eagerly*). Despite the great misery, there are still kind people. Once, when I was little, I fell down with a load of brushwood. An old man picked me up. He gave me some cheese too. I've often though of that. Especially those who don't have much to eat like to give some away. People probably like to show what they can do, and how could they show it better than by being kind? Being wicked is just being clumsy. When someone sings a song or builds a machine or plants some rice, that's really a sort of kindness. And you're kind, too.

SUN. It doesn't seem hard to be kind in your eyes.

SHEN TE. No. Just now I felt a raindrop.

SUN. Where.

SHEN TE. Between the eyes.

SUN. Nearer the right one or nearer the left?

SHEN TE. Nearer the left.

SUN. Good. (*After a while, sleepily*) And you're through with men?

SHEN TE (*smiling*). But my legs aren't crooked.

SUN. Perhaps not.

SHEN TE. Definitely not.

SUN (*tired, leaning against the tree*). I haven't eaten anything for two days or drunk anything for one. So I couldn't love you, sister, even if I wanted to.

SHEN TE. It's lovely in the rain.

(*Wang, the water seller, appears. He sings.*)

THE SONG OF THE WATER SELLER IN THE RAIN

I'm selling water, water,
And I stand here in the rain.
For such a little water
I've suffered too much pain.
And I shout: "Buy water!"
But nobody's buying
Parched and dying
And drinking and paying!
Buy water, you dogs!

O how I wish the rain would stop!
Last night in bed I dreamt again
That seven years passed without any rain.
I doled out water by the drop.
O how they shouted: "Water, water!"
Each man who came to my place
I looked him over to see whether
I really liked his face.
How their tongues hung out!

(*laughing*)
And now reclining on their backs
The little plants and such
Drink at the udder of the clouds
And never ask: How much?
And I shout: "Buy water!"
But nobody's buying
Parched and dying
And drinking and paying!
Buy water, you dogs!

(*The rain has stopped. Shen Te sees Wang and runs toward him.*)

SHEN TE. Oh, Wang, are you back again? I've got your carrying pole at home.

WANG. Thank you very much for keeping it! How are you, Shen
Te?

SHEN TE. I'm well. I've met a very clever and brave man. And
I'd like to buy a cup of your water.

WANG. Put your head back and open your mouth and you'll
have as much water as you want. The willow over there is
still dripping.

SHEN TE.

But I want your water, Wang,
The water carried from far
The water that has made you tired
The water that will be hard to sell because it is raining.
And I need it for the gentleman over there.
He is a pilot.
A pilot is bolder than other men.
In the clouds' company!
Braving the great storms
He flies through the skies
And brings to friends in far-off lands
The friendly mail.

(*She pays and runs over to Sun with the cup.*)

SHEN TE (*calling back, laughing, to Wang*). He's fallen asleep.
Despair and rain and I have made him tired.

3·A

*Wang's sleeping quarters in a sewer pipe. The water seller is
asleep. Music. The sewer pipe becomes transparent and the
Gods appear to the dreaming Wang.*

WANG (*radiantly*). I've seen her, illustrious ones! She's still the
same!

THE FIRST GOD. We're glad to hear it.

WANG. She loves! She's shown me her friend. She's really well off.

THE FIRST GOD. That's good to hear. Let's hope it will give her strength in her striving toward the good.

WANG. Absolutely! She does as many good deeds as she can.

THE FIRST GOD. What sort of good deeds? Tell us about it, my dear Wang!

WANG. She has a kind word for everyone.

THE FIRST GOD (*eagerly*). Yes, and . . . ?

WANG. It seldom happens that anyone leaves her little store without tobacco just because he has no money.

THE FIRST GOD. That doesn't sound bad. Anything else?

WANG. She gave lodging to a family of eight!

THE FIRST GOD (*triumphantly to the Second*). Eight! (*To Wang*) And something else perhaps?

WANG. She bought a cup of water from me, even though it was raining.

THE FIRST GOD. Of course, all these smaller good deeds. That's understood.

WANG. But they run into money. A little store doesn't make so much.

THE FIRST GOD. Yes, surely. But a prudent gardener can produce miracles even on a tiny plot.

WANG. She really does that! Every morning she hands out rice, and believe me, it takes more than half her earnings!

THE FIRST GOD (*a little disappointed*). I'm not saying anything. And for a beginning, I'm not dissatisfied.

WANG. Just think, times aren't exactly good! Once, her store got into difficulties and she had to call a cousin to her aid.

> As soon as there was a place that was shielded
>   from the wind
> The ruffled birds of the whole wintry sky
> Came flying and fought for the place
> And the hungry fox bit through the thin wall
> And the one-legged wolf tipped the small dish over.

In short, she couldn't manage all the business herself any

more. But they all agree that she's a good girl. Everywhere she's called the Angel of the Suburbs already. So much good comes from her store. Whatever the carpenter Lin To may say!

THE FIRST GOD. What does that mean? Does the carpenter Lin To speak badly of her?

WANG. Oh, he only says that the shelves in the store weren't paid for in full.

THE SECOND GOD. What are you saying now? A carpenter wasn't paid? In Shen Te's store? How could she allow that?

WANG. I guess she didn't have the money.

THE SECOND GOD. All the same one pays what one owes. The mere appearance of injustice has to be avoided. First the letter of the commandment must be fulfilled. Then the spirit.

WANG. But it was only her cousin, illustrious one, not she herself!

THE SECOND GOD. Then that cousin must never cross her threshold again!

WANG (*downcast*). I understand, illustrious one! In defense of Shen Te, let me at least say that her cousin is considered a highly respectable businessman. Even the police value him.

THE FIRST GOD. Well, we don't want to damn this cousin without having heard him. I admit I don't understand anything about business. Perhaps one should make inquiries to find out what is customary. But anyway, business — is it so very necessary? They're always doing business nowadays! Did the Seven Good Kings do business? Did the Kung the Just sell fish? What does business have to do with an honest and dignified life?

THE SECOND GOD (*with a bad cold*). In any case such a thing must not happen again. (*He turns to go. The two other Gods turn too.*)

THE THIRD GOD (*the last to turn away, embarrassed*). You must forgive our harsh tone today. We're over-tired and haven't slept enough. Lodgings for the night! The wealthy give us the very best of recommendations to the poor, but the poor don't have enough room.

THE GODS (*moving away, grumbling*). Weak, the best of them! Nothing decisive! Little, little! Everything from the heart, of course, but it doesn't amount to much! At least, she should see that . . .

(*One no longer hears them.*)

WANG (*calling after them*). Oh, don't be angry, illustrious ones! Don't ask too much all at once!

4

The square in front of Shen Te's tobacco store. A barber's shop, a carpet store, and Shen Te's tobacco store. It is morning. In front of Shen Te's store, two of the family of eight, the Grand-father and the Sister-in-law, are waiting. Waiting also are the Unemployed and Mrs. Shin.

THE SISTER-IN-LAW. She didn't come home last night!

MRS. SHIN. Unbelievable behavior! At last this crazy cousin has gone away and madam deigns, now and then at least, to give us a little bit of rice out of all her abundance. But already she's staying out all night, loitering around, God knows where!

(*Loud voices are heard from the barber's. Wang stumbles out, followed by the fat barber, Mr. Shu Fu, who is carrying a heavy curling iron.*)

MR. SHU FU. I'll teach you to bother my customers with your smelly water! Take your cup and get going!

(*Wang reaches for the cup held out by Mr. Shu Fu, who hits him on the hand with the curling iron. Wang cries out with pain.*)

MR. SHU FU. There you have it! Let it be a lesson to you! (*He goes puffing back into his store.*)

THE UNEMPLOYED (*picking up the cup and handing it to Wang*). You can report him to the police for hitting you like that.

WANG. My hand's smashed.

THE UNEMPLOYED. Is something broken?

WANG. I can't move it.

THE UNEMPLOYED. Sit down and pour a little water over it! (*Wang sits down.*)

MRS. SHIN. You get the water cheap, anyway.

THE SISTER-IN-LAW. You can't even get a little linen rag here at eight in the morning. She's got to go out! Adventures! What a scandal!

MRS. SHIN (*gloomily*). She's forgotten us!

(*Shen Te comes down the street carrying a dish of rice.*)

SHEN TE (*to the audience*). I've never seen the town in the early morning before. At this hour I used to lie in bed with a dirty blanket over my head, afraid of waking up. Today I walked among the newspaper boys, among the men who rinse the pavement with water, and among the ox carts that bring fresh vegetables from the country. I've walked a long way from Sun's neighborhood over here, but I've been getting merrier at every step. I've always been told that if you're in love you walk on clouds, but the best thing is walking on the earth, on the pavement. I tell you, in the morning rows of houses look like rubbish heaps with lights on them. The sky is pink and transparent because there's no dust yet. I tell you, you miss much if you don't love, if you don't see your Setzuan at the hour when it rises from sleep like a sober old craftsman pumping his lungs full of fresh air and reaching for his tools, as the poets say. (*To the waiting people*) Good morning! Here's the rice! (*She distributes the rice, then notices Wang.*) Good morning, Wang. I'm quite light-headed today. On the way home I looked at myself in every shop window, and now I feel like buying a shawl. (*After hesitating a little*) I'd so much like to be beautiful. (*She quickly goes into the carpet store.*)

MR. SHU FU (*who has stepped out again, to the audience*). I'm quite surprised to note how beautiful Miss Shen Te looks today. She's the owner of the tobacco store across the street and I've never really noticed her before. I've been looking at her for three minutes and I think I'm already in love with her. An incredibly attractive person! (*To Wang*) Clear off, you rascal! (*He goes back into his store. Shen Te, the Old Woman, and her husband the carpet dealer step out of the carpet store. Shen Te is wearing a shawl, the carpet dealer is holding out a mirror.*)

THE OLD WOMAN. It's very pretty and not expensive because it has a little hole at the bottom.

SHEN TE (*looking at the shawl on the Old Woman's arm*). The green one's nice too.

THE OLD WOMAN (*smiling*). But unfortunately not the least bit damaged.

SHEN TE. Yes, that's a shame. I can't spend too much, with my small store. I only take in a little and the expenses are great.

THE OLD WOMAN. It's good deeds that cost you so much. Be careful. In the beginning, every dish of rice counts, doesn't it?

SHEN TE (*trying on the shawl with the little hole in it*). Well, that's how things are. But at the moment I'm light-headed. I wonder if this color suits me?

THE OLD WOMAN. That's a question to put to a *man*.

SHEN TE (*turning to the Old Man*). Does it suit me?

THE OLD MAN. Why don't you ask . . .

SHEN TE (*very politely*). No, I'm asking you.

THE OLD MAN (*also politely*). The shawl suits you. But wear it with the dull side turned out.

(*Shen Te pays.*)

THE OLD WOMAN. If you don't like it, you can always exchange it. (*She pulls her aside.*) Does he have any money?

SHEN TE (*laughing*). Oh no!

THE OLD WOMAN. Then how will you be able to pay the rent?

SHEN TE. The rent? I'd completely forgotten it!

THE OLD WOMAN. I thought as much. And next Monday is the first of the month. I'd like to talk something over with you.

You know, my husband and I had a few doubts about the marriage ad after we got to know you. We decided to help you out if it comes to the worst. We've put aside a little money and can lend you two hundred silver dollars. If you wish you can pledge us your stock of tobacco. Of course we don't need a written agreement.

SHEN TE. Do you really want to lend money to a light-headed person like me?

THE OLD WOMAN. Well, to be honest, we might not lend it to your cousin — who's definitely not light-headed. But we don't worry about lending it to you.

THE OLD MAN (*stepping up to them*). Settled?

SHEN TE. I wish the gods could have heard your wife just now, Mr. Ma. They're looking for good people who're happy. And you must be happy helping me, for it was love that got me into trouble.

(*The old couple smile at each other.*)

THE OLD MAN. Here's the money.

(*He hands her an envelope. Shen Te takes it and bows. The old couple bow too. They go back into their store.*)

SHEN TE (*to Wang, holding up her envelope*). This is the rent for half a year! Isn't it just like a miracle? And how do you like my new shawl, Wang?

WANG. Did you buy it for the fellow I saw in the city park?

(*Shen Te nods.*)

MRS. SHIN. Maybe you better take a look at his smashed hand? Never mind telling him your doubtful adventures!

SHEN TE (*taken aback*). What's the matter with your hand?

MRS. SHIN. The barber smashed it with a curling iron in front of our eyes.

SHEN TE (*horrified at her negligence*). And I didn't notice anything! You must go to the doctor this minute or your hand will get stiff and you'll never be able to work properly again. What a terrible misfortune! Quick, get up! Go, quickly!

THE UNEMPLOYED. It's not the doctor he should go to but the judge! He can demand compensation from the barber, he's rich.

43

WANG. You think there's a chance?

MRS. SHIN. If it's really smashed. But is it?

WANG. I think so. It's swollen up already. Maybe I could get a pension?

MRS. SHIN. Of course you've got to have a witness.

WANG. But you *all* saw it! You could *all* testify?

(*He looks round. The Unemployed, the Grandfather, and the Sister-in-law sit by the wall of the house and eat. Nobody looks up.*)

SHEN TE (*to Mrs. Shin*). But you saw it yourself!

MRS. SHIN. I don't want anything to do with the police.

SHEN TE (*to the Sister-in-law*). What about you?

THE SISTER-IN-LAW. Me? I wasn't looking!

MRS. SHIN. Of course you were! I saw you! But you're afraid because the barber's a big shot.

SHEN TE (*to the Grandfather*). I'm sure *you'll* testify!

THE SISTER-IN-LAW. His testimony won't be accepted. He's gaga.

SHEN TE (*to the Unemployed*). It might be a matter of a pension for life.

THE UNEMPLOYED. I've been picked up twice for begging. *My* testimony would only do him harm.

SHEN TE (*not quite believing*). So none of you want to say what happened? His hand was smashed in broad daylight, all of you were watching, and nobody wants to speak! (*Angrily*)

Unhappy men!
Your brother is assaulted and you shut your eyes!
He is hit and cries aloud and you are silent?
The beast prowls, chooses his victim, and you say:
He's spared us because we do not show displeasure.
What sort of a city is this? What sort of people
    are you?
When injustice is done there should be revolt
    in the city.
And if there is no revolt, it were better that the
    city should perish in fire before night falls!

Wang, if no one present will be your witness, I will. I'll say *I* saw it.

44

MRS. SHIN. That'll be perjury.

WANG. I don't know if I can accept this. Though maybe I'll have to. (*Looking at his hand, worried*) Do you think it's swollen enough? I think maybe the swelling's gone down now?

THE UNEMPLOYED (*reassuring him*). No, the swelling definitely hasn't gone down.

WANG. Hasn't it? No, I guess it's *more* swollen, if anything. Maybe my wrist is broken after all! I'd better run to the judge this minute.

(*Carefully holding his hand and looking at it all the time, he runs off. Mrs. Shin runs into the barber's shop.*)

THE UNEMPLOYED. She wants to get on the right side of the barber.

THE SISTER-IN-LAW. We can't change the world.

SHEN TE (*discouraged*). I didn't want to scold you. I'm only afraid. No, I *did* want to scold. Get out of my sight!

(*The Unemployed, the Sister-in-law, and the Grandfather go off, eating and sulking.*)

SHEN TE (*to the audience*).

> They no longer answer.
> Where one puts them they stay
> And if one sends them away
> They quickly go.
> Nothing moves their hearts.
> Only the smell of food can make them look up.

(*An oldish woman comes running in.*)

THE OLDISH WOMAN (*out of breath*). Are you Miss Shen Te? My son. Has told me everything. I am. Sun's mother, Mrs. Yang. Just think, he has. A chance now. To get a job as flier. This morning. Just now a letter. Came from Peking. From the manager of the airmail service.

SHEN TE. He can fly again? Oh, Mrs. Yang!

MRS. YANG. But the job. Costs a lot of money. Five hundred silver dollars.

SHEN TE. That's a lot, but money mustn't stand in the way of a thing like that. After all, I've got the store!

MRS. YANG. If you could only do something!

SHEN TE (*embracing her*). If only I could!

MRS. YANG. You would give a talented young man a chance?

SHEN TE. How can they prevent a man from being useful? (*After a pause*) Only I won't get enough for the store, and these two hundred silver dollars cash are just borrowed. Take them with you at once. I'll pay them back by selling my tobacco stock. (*She gives her the old couple's money.*)

MRS. YANG. Oh, Miss Shen Te, that really is help at the right moment! And they were calling him the Dead Flier of Setzuan, they were all so convinced he'd never do any more flying!

SHEN TE. But we need three hundred silver dollars more for the job. We've got to think, Mrs. Yang. (*Slowly*) I know someone who might be able to help me. Someone who helped me out once before. I didn't really want to call him again, he's so hard and cunning. It would certainly have to be the last time. But a flier's got to fly, that's clear.

(*Distant sound of engines.*)

MRS. YANG. If the man you're talking about could get the money! Look, that's the morning mail plane, going to Peking!

SHEN TE (*decisively*). Wave, Mrs. Yang! I'm sure the pilot can see us! (*She waves with her shawl.*) You wave too!

MRS. YANG (*waving*). You know the pilot who's flying up there?

SHEN TE. No. I know the pilot who *shall* be up there. He gave up hope but he *shall* fly, Mrs. Yang. One at least shall raise himself above this misery and above us all! (*To the audience*)

> Yang Sun, my lover,
> In the clouds' company!
> Braving the great storms
> Flying through the skies
> And bringing to friends in distant lands
> The friendly mail.

4·A

Before the curtain. Shen Te appears with the suit and mask of Shui Ta in her hands. She sings.

THE SONG OF THE DEFENSELESSNESS OF
THE GODS AND GOOD MEN

In our country
The useful man needs luck.
Only if he finds strong helpers
Can he prove himself useful.
Good men can't help themselves
And the gods are powerless.
Why don't the gods have mines and cannon
Battleships, bombers, and tanks?
Bring down the bad and save the good?
Shouldn't we all give thanks?

(She puts on Shui Ta's suit and takes a few steps in his manner.)

Good men
Cannot long remain good in our country.
Where plates are empty, the diners fight.
Alas, the commandments of the gods
Are no use against want.
Why don't the gods appear in our markets
And, smiling, distribute the plentiful food?
Let every man eat and drink at his pleasure
And be to his brother loving and good?

(She puts on the mask of Shui Ta and now sings with his voice.)

To procure a dinner
You must be hard as builders of empire.
Without trampling down twelve others
You cannot help one poor man.

47

Why then don't the gods speak up in their heaven
And say that they owe the good world to good men?
Why don't they stand by good men with their bombers
Fire their guns and suffer no suffering then?

5

*The tobacco store. Shui Ta sits behind the counter reading the
paper. He doesn't pay the least attention to Mrs. Shin, who is
cleaning up and talking at the same time.*

MRS. SHIN. A little store like this soon comes to ruin when certain rumors start spreading in the neighborhood. Believe me.
It's high time that a decent man like you started looking into this dubious affair between Miss Shen Te and that Yang
Sun from Yellow Street. Don't forget Mr. Shu Fu, the barber
next door, a man with twelve houses and only one wife, and
she's old, only yesterday confessed a certain interest in Miss
Shen Te. A very flattering interest, I thought. He even in-
quired about her means. And that, if I may say so, proves
real affection.
*(Since she gets no answer, she finally goes out with the
bucket.)*
SUN'S VOICE *(from outside)*. Is that Miss Shen Te's store?
MRS. SHIN'S VOICE. Yes, this is it. But today her cousin's here.
*(With the light steps of Shen Te, Shui Ta runs to a mirror.
She is just about to start fixing her hair when she notices the
mistake in the mirror. She turns away laughing softly. Enter
Yang Sun. Behind him comes the inquisitive Mrs. Shin. She
goes past him into the back room.)*
SUN. I'm Yang Sun. *(Shui Ta bows.)* Is Shen Te here?
SHUI TA. No, she's not.

SUN. I guess you know what our relationship is? (*He begins to inspect the store.*) A real live store! I always thought she was just talking big. (*He looks with satisfaction into the little boxes and china jars.*) Man, I'm going to fly again! (*He takes a cigar and Shui Ta gives him a light.*) D'you think we can squeeze another three hundred silver dollars out of the store?

SHUI TA. May I ask if you intend to sell it right away?

SUN. Well, do we have the three hundred in cash? (*Shui Ta shakes his head.*) It was decent of her to come right out with the two hundred. But with three hundred still missing, they won't be much use.

SHUI TA. Perhaps it was rather rash of her to promise you the money. It may cost her the store. Haste, they say, is the name of the wind that knocks down the scaffolding.

SUN. I need the money quickly or not at all. And the girl isn't one to keep you waiting either. For one thing or another, you get me?

SHUI TA. I get you.

SUN. Uh-huh.

SHUI TA. May I know what the five hundred silver dollars will be used for?

SUN. Sure. I see I'm to be sounded out. The manager at the Peking airport is a friend of mine from flying school. He can get me the job if I cough up five hundred silver dollars.

SHUI TA. Is not that sum unusually high?

SUN. No. He'll have to fire one of his present pilots. For negligence. And the fellow he has in mind isn't negligent, because he's got a large family. You understand. All this, by the way, in confidence. Shen Te needn't know it.

SHUI TA. Perhaps not. Just one thing — won't that manager sell *you* out next month?

SUN. Not me. There won't be any negligence in my work. I was unemployed long enough.

SHUI TA (*nodding*). The hungry dog pulls the cart home faster. (*He scrutinizes him.*) The responsibility is very great. Mr. Yang Sun, you ask my cousin to give up her small posses-

49

sions, to leave all her friends in this town, and to put her entire fate into your hands. I assume you intend to marry Shen Te?

SUN. I'd be prepared to.

SHUI TA. But isn't it a pity, then, to get rid of the store for a few silver dollars? We won't get much for it if we have to sell at once. The two hundred silver dollars you have in your hands would pay the rent for half a year. Wouldn't that tempt you to continue in the tobacco business?

SUN. Would it tempt *me*? Is Yang Sun, the flier, to be seen standing behind the counter: "Do you wish a strong cigar or a mild one, worthy sir?" That's no business for the Yang Sun's, not in this century!

SHUI TA. Allow me to ask, is flying very profitable?

SUN (*pulling a letter out of his pocket*). Sir, I'd get two hundred and fifty silver dollars a month! Look at the letter yourself. Here's the stamp and the postmark. Peking.

SHUI TA. Two hundred and fifty silver dollars? That's a lot.

SUN. Do you think I fly for nothing?

SHUI TA. The job seems to be good. Mr. Yang Sun, my cousin has commissioned me to help you to this post which means so much to you. From her own point of view, I cannot see any good reason why she shouldn't follow the inclinations of her heart. She has every right to experience the joys of love. I'm prepared to turn everything here to money. Here comes the landlady, Mrs. Mi Tzu, whom I'll ask to advise me about the sale.

THE LANDLADY (*entering*). Good day, Mr. Shui Ta. I suppose it's about the rent which is due the day after tomorrow?

SHUI TA. Mrs. Mi Tzu, circumstances have arisen which make it look doubtful whether my cousin will keep her store. She's planning to marry, and her future husband (*he introduces Yang Sun*), Mr. Yang Sun, will take her to Peking where they are to start a new life. If I can get enough for my tobacco, I shall sell out.

THE LANDLADY. How much do you need?

SUN. Three hundred down.

SHUI TA (*quickly*). No, five hundred!

THE LANDLADY (*to Sun*). Perhaps I'll be able to help you. How much did your tobacco cost?

SHUI TA. My cousin paid a thousand silver dollars for it and very little has been sold.

THE LANDLADY. A thousand silver dollars! She was gypped of course. I'll tell you something: I'll pay you three hundred silver dollars for the whole store if you move out the day after tomorrow.

SUN. We'll do that. It'll work, old man!

SHUI TA. It's too little.

SUN. It's enough!

SHUI TA. I've got to have at least five hundred.

SUN. What for?

SHUI TA (*to the Landlady*). Allow me to talk something over with my cousin's fiancé. (*Aside to Sun*) All the tobacco here has been pledged to two old people for the two hundred silver dollars which were given to you yesterday.

SUN. Is there a written agreement?

SHUI TA. No.

SUN (*to the Landlady*). We can manage with three hundred.

THE LANDLADY. But I've got to know whether the store is in debt.

SUN. You answer!

SHUI TA. The store is not in debt.

SUN. When can the three hundred be had?

THE LANDLADY. The day after tomorrow, and you can still think it over. You'll get more if you don't sell in such a rush. I'll pay three hundred, but only because I want to do my share in what seems to be a case of young love. (*Exit.*)

SUN (*calling after her*). We'll make the deal! Little boxes, jars and sacks, everything for three hundred and the pain's over. (*To Shui Ta*) Perhaps some other place we can get more by the day after tomorrow?

SHUI TA. Not in such a short time. We won't have one silver dollar apart from the three hundred of Mrs. Mi Tzu. You have the money for the trip and the first few weeks?

SUN. Sure.

SHUI TA. How much is that?

SUN. I'll dig it up, anyway, even if I have to steal it!

SHUI TA. Oh, I see, this money too has to be dug up?

SUN. Don't fall out of your shoes, old man, I'll get to Peking somehow.

SHUI TA. It can't be so cheap for two people.

SUN. *Two* people? I'm leaving the girl behind. At first, she'll only be a millstone round my neck.

SHUI TA. I see.

SUN. Why d'you look at me as if I was a leaking oil tank? You've got to manage the best you can.

SHUI TA. And how is my cousin to live?

SUN. Can't *you* do something for her?

SHUI TA. I'll try. (*pause*) I wish, Mr. Yang Sun, you'd hand over to me the two hundred silver dollars and would leave them here till you can show me two tickets to Peking.

SUN. My dear man, I wish you'd mind your own business.

SHUI TA. Miss Shen Te . . .

SUN. Just leave the girl to me.

SHUI TA. . . . might not want to sell her store when she learns that . . .

SUN. She'll want to. Even then.

SHUI TA. And you're not afraid of my interference?

SUN. My dear sir!

SHUI TA. You seem to forget she's a human being and has got some sense.

SUN (*amused*). What certain people think about their female relatives and the effect of reasonable persuasion has always been a source of wonder to me. Have you ever heard of the power of love? The tickling of the flesh? You want to talk reason to her? She doesn't know what reason is! On the other hand, the poor creature's been abused all her life. I've only to put my hand on her shoulder and say "you're coming with me" and she hears bells and wouldn't know her own mother.

SHUI TA (*with difficulty*). Mr. Yang Sun!

SUN. Mr. What's-your-name!

52

SHUI TA. My cousin is devoted to you because . . .

SUN. Shall we say because I've got my hand on her bosom? Put that in your pipe and smoke it! (*He takes another cigar, then puts a few in his pocket, and finally takes the whole box under his arm.*) Don't you go to her with empty hands. We'll stick to the marriage. And she'll bring the three hundred or you'll bring them. Either she or you! (*Exit.*)

MRS. SHIN (*putting her head out of the back room*). Not exactly pleasant. And all of Yellow Street knows he's got the girl completely under his thumb.

SHUI TA (*crying out*). The store's gone! He isn't in love! I'm lost! (*He begins to run round like an imprisoned animal, repeating,* "The store's gone!" *until he stops suddenly and begins to talk to Mrs. Shin.*) Shin, you grew up in the gutter and so did I. Are we frivolous? No. Do we lack the necessary brutality? No. I'm ready to take you by the throat and shake you till you spit out the last crumb of cheese you've stolen from me. You know that. The times are terrible, this town is hell, but gradually we manage to crawl up the smooth walls. Then bad luck overtakes one or another of us: he is in love. That's enough, he's lost. One weakness and you're finished. How are you to free yourself of *all* weaknesses, and especially of the deadliest of weaknesses, love? Love is absolutely impossible! It's much too expensive! But then, tell me yourself, can one live and be *always* on the watch? What sort of a world is this?

> Caresses turn to strangulation.
> The sigh of love turns to a cry of fear.
> Why are the vultures circling over there?
> A girl is going to meet her lover.

MRS. SHIN. I think I better go and get the barber right away. You've got to talk with the barber. He's a man of honor. The barber, he's the right one for your cousin.
(*Receiving no answer, she runs off. Shui Ta runs around again until Mr. Shu Fu enters, followed by Mrs. Shin, who, however, on a sign from Mr. Shu Fu, is forced to withdraw.*)

SHUI TA (*hurrying toward him*). My dear sir, I know from

hearsay that you have hinted at a certain interest in my cousin. Let me set aside all the laws of propriety and reserve: Miss Shen Te is at the moment in great danger.

MR. SHU FU. Oh!

SHUI TA. Only a few hours ago the possessor of her own store, my cousin is now little more than a beggar. Mr. Shu Fu, this store is ruined.

MR. SHU FU. Mr. Shui Ta, the charm of Miss Shen Te lies not in the goodness of her store but in the goodness of her heart. The name which this neighborhood has given to the young lady tells all. They call her the Angel of the Suburbs!

SHUI TA. My dear sir, this goodness has cost my cousin two hundred silver dollars on a single day. We have to put a stop to that.

MR. SHU FU. Allow me to express a different opinion: we've got to open the gates wide to this goodness. It's in the nature of the young lady to do good. Every morning I affectionately watch her feeding four people. What does that signify? Why can't she feed four hundred? I hear, for instance, that she's racking her brains about how to shelter some homeless people. My cabins behind the cattle run are empty. They're at her disposal. And so on and so forth . . . Mr. Shui Ta, might I hope that Miss Shen Te would lend an ear to certain ideas which have come to me in the last few days? Ideas like these?

SHUI TA. Mr. Shu Fu, she will listen to such high thoughts with admiration.

(*Enter Wang with the Policeman. Mr. Shu Fu turns around and studies the shelves.*)

WANG. Is Miss Shen Te here?

SHUI TA. No.

WANG. I am Wang, the water seller. I guess you're Mr. Shui Ta?

SHUI TA. Quite right. Good day, Wang.

WANG. I'm a friend of Shen Te's.

SHUI TA. You're one of her oldest friends, I know.

WANG (*to the Policeman*). You see? (*To Shui Ta*) I'm coming because of my hand.

THE POLICEMAN. It's smashed all right. There's no doubt about it.

SHUI TA (*quickly*). I see you need a sling. (*He gets a shawl from the back room and throws it to Wang.*)

WANG. But that's her new shawl.

SHUI TA. She no longer needs it.

WANG. But she bought it to please a certain person.

SHUI TA. As things have turned out, that is no longer necessary.

WANG (*making himself a sling out of the shawl*). She's my only witness.

THE POLICEMAN. Your cousin's supposed to've seen how the barber Shu Fu hit the water seller with the curling iron. D'you know anything about it?

SHUI TA. I only know that my cousin wasn't present when the incident occurred.

WANG. That's a misunderstanding! Just wait till Shen Te's here and everything will be cleared up. Shen Te'll bear witness to everything. Where is she?

SHUI TA (*seriously*). Mr. Wang, you call yourself my cousin's friend. My cousin has a lot of worries right now. She's been terribly exploited from all sides. In the future, she won't be able to afford the smallest weakness. I'm convinced you won't ask her to lose all she has by making her say anything but the truth in this matter.

WANG (*confused*). But *she* advised me to go to the judge.

SHUI TA. Was the judge supposed to heal your hand? (*Mr. Shu Fu turns round.*) Mr. Wang, it's one of my principles never to meddle in the quarrels of my friends. (*Shui Ta bows to Mr. Shu Fu who returns the bow.*)

WANG (*taking off the sling and putting it back, sadly*). I understand.

THE POLICEMAN. And now I guess I can go again. You went to a decent man — the wrong fellow for your swindling. You better be a bit more careful next time, with your accusations. If Mr. Shu Fu didn't put mercy before justice, you could be jailed for libel. Off with you now.

(*Exeunt.*)

55

SHUI TA. I beg you to excuse this occurrence.

MR. SHU FU. It's excused. (*Urgently*) And this affair with a "certain person" (*he points to the shawl*) is really over? Completely finished?

SHUI TA. Completely. She's seen through him. Of course, it'll take time till she's got over everything.

MR. SHU FU. We shall be careful. Delicate.

SHUI TA. There are some fresh wounds.

MR. SHU FU. She'll go to the country.

SHUI TA. For some weeks. However, before that she'll be glad to talk everything over with someone she can trust.

MR. SHU FU. At a small dinner in a small but good restaurant.

SHUI TA. In a discreet way. I'll hurry to inform my cousin. She'll be reasonable. She's very worried about the store, which she regards as a gift of the gods. Be patient for a few minutes. (*Exit into the back room.*)

MRS. SHIN (*putting her head in*). May I congratulate you?

MR. SHU FU. Mrs. Shin, you may let Miss Shen Te's protégés know today that I am giving them shelter in the cabins behind the cattle run.

(*She nods, grinning.*)

MR. SHU FU (*getting up, to the audience*). What do you think of me, ladies and gentlemen? Could anyone do more? Could anyone be less selfish? More farsighted? A small dinner! What vulgar and clumsy thoughts this would bring into the minds of most people. But nothing like that will happen. Nothing. She won't be touched. Not even casually. Not even accidentally while passing the salt! Nothing but ideas will be exchanged. Two souls will find each other over the flowers on the table, white chrysanthemums by the way. (*He makes a note of that.*) No, we won't exploit an unfortunate situation. We won't turn a disappointment to our advantage. Understanding and assistance will be offered. And almost without a sound. A single glance might perhaps acknowledge it. A glance which could also mean more.

MRS. SHIN. So everything went as you wished, Mr. Shu Fu?

MR. SHU FU. Oh, just as I wished! There'll presumably be a few changes in this district. A certain person has been shown the door and some of the plots against this shop will be spoiled. Certain people who still dare to harm the reputation of the chastest girl in this city will get into trouble with me in the future. What do you know about this Yang Sun?

MRS. SHIN. He's the dirtiest, laziest . . .

MR. SHU FU. He's nothing. He doesn't exist. He can't be found, Mrs. Shin.

(*Enter Sun.*)

SUN. What's going on here?

MRS. SHIN. Mr. Shu Fu, d'you want me to call Mr. Shui Ta? He won't want strangers loitering around in the store.

MR. SHU FU. Miss Shen Te is having an important talk with Mr. Shui Ta and mustn't be interrupted.

SUN. What, she's here? I didn't see her go in! What sort of a talk is that? I've got to be in on it!

MR. SHU FU (*preventing him from going into the back room*). You'll have to be patient, my dear sir. I think I know who you are. Please take note that Miss Shen Te and I are about to announce our engagement.

SUN. What?

MRS. SHIN. That surprises you, doesn't it?

(*Sun is fighting with the barber to get into the back room when Shen Te steps out of it.*)

MR. SHU FU. Excuse me, dear Shen Te. Perhaps you could explain . . .

SUN. What's the matter, Shen Te? Are you crazy?

SHEN TE (*breathlessly*). Sun, my cousin and Mr. Shu Fu have come to an agreement: I'm to listen to Mr. Shu Fu's ideas about how to help the people of the neighborhood. (*pause*) My cousin wants to part us.

SUN. And you agree?

SHEN TE. Yes.

(*Pause.*)

SUN. Did they tell you I'm a bad man?

(*Shen Te is silent.*)

SUN. Maybe I *am* a bad man, Shen Te. And that's why I need

you. I'm low. Without money, without manners. But I fight back. They're driving you into misfortune, Shen Te. (*He goes over to her and speaks in an undertone.*) Just look at him! Do you have no eyes in your head? (*With his hand on her shoulder*) Poor creature, *now* what did they want you to do? Make a reasonable match! Without me they'd just have sacrificed you. Admit that, but for me, you would have gone away with him!

SHEN TE. Yes.

SUN. A man you don't love.

SHEN TE. Yes.

SUN. Have you forgotten everything? How it was raining?

SHEN TE. No.

SUN. How you cut me from the tree? How you bought me a cup of water? How you promised me the money so I could fly again?

SHEN TE (*trembling*). What do you want?

SUN. I want you to come with me.

SHEN TE. Mr. Shu Fu, forgive me, I want to go away with Sun.

SUN. We're lovers, you know. (*He leads her to the door.*) Where is the key to the store? (*He takes it from her pocket and hands it to Mrs. Shin.*) Leave it outside the door when you're through. Come on, Shen Te.

MR. SHU FU. But this is rape! (*Shouting to the back*) Mr. Shui Ta!

SUN. Tell him not to shout so much in here.

SHEN TE. Please don't call my cousin, Mr. Shu Fu. He doesn't agree with me, I know. But he's not right, I can feel it. (*To the audience*)

> I want to go with the one I love
> I don't want to reckon what it will cost
> I don't want to consider if it is wise
> I want to go with the one I love.

SUN. That's it.

(*Exeunt.*)

Before the curtain. Shen Te, in her wedding outfit and on the way to her wedding, turns to the audience.

SHEN TE. I've had a terrible experience. As I was stepping out of the house, gay and full of expectation, the carpet dealer's old wife was standing on the street. She was trembling all over, and she told me that her husband had fallen sick from excitement and worry about the money they'd lent me. She thought it best that I return the money to her now in any case. Of course I promised it to her. She was very relieved, wished me the best of luck with tears in her eyes and asked me to forgive her because she couldn't altogether trust my cousin, nor, unfortunately, Sun. I had to sit down when she'd gone, I was so alarmed by my own behavior. With my emotions in an uproar, I threw myself again into the arms of Yang Sun. I couldn't resist his voice and his caresses. The bad things he said to Shui Ta didn't teach Shen Te anything. Sinking into his arms, I thought: the gods wanted me to be good to myself too.

> To let no one perish, not even one's self,
> To fill everyone with happiness, even one's self,
> That is good.

How could I simply forget those two good old people? Like a small hurricane, Sun just swept away my store and all my friends in the direction of Peking. But he's not bad and he loves me. As long as I'm with him, he won't do anything bad. What men say between themselves doesn't count. He just wants to seem big and powerful and above all hard-boiled. When I tell him that the old couple won't be able to pay their taxes, he'll understand everything. He'd rather go and work in the cement factory than owe his flying to a crime. Of course flying's a great passion with Sun. Shall I be strong enough to bring out the good in him? Now, on the way to my wedding, I waver between fear and joy. (*She goes quickly off.*)

6

A side room of a cheap restaurant in the suburbs. A waiter pours out wine for the wedding party. Near Shen Te are the Grandfather, the Sister-in-law, the Niece, Mrs. Shin, and the Unemployed. In the corner, alone, stands a Priest. Down stage, Sun is talking with his mother, Mrs. Yang. He is wearing a dinner jacket.

SUN. Something unpleasant, Mamma. She just told me in all innocence that she can't sell the store for me. Somebody or other is bringing a claim because they lent her the two hundred silver dollars which she gave to you. And her cousin said that there wasn't any written agreement.

MRS. YANG. What did you say to her? Of course you can't marry her now.

SUN. There's no sense in talking with her about these things. She's got a thick head. I've sent for her cousin.

MRS. YANG. But he wants to marry her to the barber.

SUN. I've put an end to that marriage. The barber's been insulted. Her cousin will soon understand that if I don't hand over the two hundred, the creditors will seize the store and the store will be gone, but if I don't get the three hundred, my job will be gone too.

MRS. YANG. I'll look for him outside the restaurant. Go to your bride, now, Sun!

SHEN TE (*pouring wine, to the audience*). I wasn't mistaken in him. I couldn't see a trace of disappointment in his face.

60

He's perfectly cheerful though it must be a heavy blow for him to have to give up flying. I love him very much. (*She waves Sun over.*) Sun, you haven't drunk a toast with the bride!

SUN. What shall we drink to?

SHEN TE. Let's drink to the future.

(*They drink.*)

SUN. When the bridegroom's tuxedo will no longer be borrowed!

SHEN TE. But when the bride's dress will still get rained on now and then.

SUN. To everything we wish for!

SHEN TE. That it may quickly come true!

MRS. YANG (*on the way out, to Mrs. Shin*). I'm delighted with my son. I've always impressed it on him that he can get whoever he wants. Why, he's a trained mechanic and flier. And what does he tell me now? "I'm marrying for love, Mamma," he says, "money isn't everything." It's a love match! (*To the Sister-in-law*) It has to happen once, hasn't it? But it's hard for a mother, it's hard. (*Calling back to the Priest*) Don't cut it too short. If you take as much time for the ceremony as you took to haggle about the price, it'll be dignified all right. (*To Shen Te*) We've got to postpone things a little still, my dear. One of our most beloved guests hasn't arrived yet. (*To all*) Excuse me, please. (*Exit.*)

THE SISTER-IN-LAW. We'll gladly be patient as long as there's wine.

(*They all sit down.*)

THE UNEMPLOYED. We're not missing anything.

SUN (*loud and jokingly before the guests*). And before the marriage I've still got to give you a little quiz. A not unnecessary thing when a wedding is held at such short notice. (*To the guests*) I've no idea what sort of a wife I'm getting. That worries me. (*To Shen Te*) For instance, can you make five cups of tea with three tea leaves?

SHEN TE. No.

SUN. I see I won't be getting any tea. Can you sleep on a sack of straw the size of the book the priest is reading?

SHEN TE. With someone else?

SUN. Alone.

SHEN TE. In that case, no.

SUN. I'm horrified at the wife I'm getting.

(*They all laugh. Behind Shen Te, Mrs. Yang steps into the doorway. With a shrug of her shoulders, she tells Sun that there's no sign of the expected guest.*)

MRS. YANG (*to the Priest, who has shown her his watch*). Don't be in such a hurry. It can be a matter of minutes. I can see they're drinking and smoking and no one's in a hurry. (*She sits down by the guests.*)

SHEN TE. Don't we have to talk about how we're going to arrange everything?

MRS. YANG. Oh, please, let's not talk shop. Shoptalk introduces a *common* note into the celebration, doesn't it?

(*The entrance bell rings. They all look to the door but nobody enters.*)

SHEN TE. Who's your mother waiting for, Sun?

SUN. That's a surprise for you. By the way, how's your cousin Shui Ta? I got on with him. A very sensible man! What a brain! Why don't you say anything?

SHEN TE. I don't know. I don't want to think of him.

SUN. Why not?

SHEN TE. Because you *shouldn't* get on well with him. If you love me, you can't love him.

SUN. Then may the three devils fetch him: the Fog-devil, the Engine-trouble-devil, and the Empty-gas-tank devil! Drink, you stubborn girl! (*He makes her drink.*)

THE SISTER-IN-LAW (*to Mrs. Shin*). Something's wrong here.

MRS. SHIN. What else did you expect?

THE PRIEST (*resolutely stepping up to Mrs. Yang, a watch in his hand*). I've got to go, Mrs. Yang. I've got another wedding to attend to, and tomorrow morning a funeral.

MRS. YANG. D'you think I like all this postponing? We were hoping to manage with one pitcher of wine. But look how it's coming to an end! (*Loudly to Shen Te*) My dear Shen Te, I can't understand where your cousin can be all this time!

62

SHEN TE. My cousin?

MRS. YANG. But, my dear, it's him we're waiting for! I'm just old fashioned enough to think that such a close relative of the bride should be present at the wedding.

SHEN TE. Oh Sun, is it because of the three hundred silver dollars?

SUN (*without looking at her*). Can't you hear? She's old fashioned. Well, I'm considerate. We'll wait another fifteen minutes and if he hasn't come then because the three devils have got him, we'll start!

MRS. YANG. I guess you all know already that my son is getting a job as a mail pilot. I'm very pleased about it. In these times, we have to make good money.

THE SISTER-IN-LAW. It's to be in Peking, isn't it?

MRS. YANG. Yes, in Peking.

SHEN TE. You've got to tell your mother, Sun, that Peking is out of the question.

SUN. Your cousin will tell her, if he agrees with you. Between us: I don't agree.

SHEN TE (*appalled*). Sun!

SUN. How I hate this Setzuan. What a town! Do you know what they all look like when I half close my eyes? Horses! They fret and screw their necks up: what's thundering there above them? How's that? They're no longer needed? What, their time's up already? Let them bite themselves to death in their horse town! O to get out of here!

SHEN TE. But I've promised the money to the old couple.

SUN. Yes, you told me. And since you do stupid things like that, it's lucky your cousin's coming. Drink, and leave business to us! We'll fix it up.

SHEN TE (*horrified*). But my cousin can't come.

SUN. What do you mean?

SHEN TE. He can't come!

SUN. And how do you figure our future? Tell me that.

SHEN TE. I thought you still had the two hundred silver dollars. We could return them tomorrow and keep the tobacco, which is worth a lot more. Then we'll sell it together in front of the cement factory since we can't pay the half year's rent.

SUN. Forget it! Forget it fast, sister! *I* am to stand on the street and sell tobacco to cement workers, I, Yang Sun, the flier! I'd rather run through all two hundred in one night! I'd rather throw it in the river! And your cousin knows me! I've arranged it with him. He's to bring the three hundred to the wedding.

SHEN TE. My cousin can't come.

SUN. And I thought he couldn't stay away.

SHEN TE. He can't be where I am.

SUN. How mysterious!

SHEN TE. Sun, you've got to know it: he's not your friend. I'm the one that loves you. My cousin Shui Ta doesn't love anybody. He's my friend, but he's no friend to my friends. He was thinking of the job at Peking when he agreed to your getting the old couple's money. But he won't bring you the three hundred silver dollars to the wedding.

SUN. And why not?

SHEN TE (*looking into his eyes*). He says you only bought one ticket to Peking.

SUN. Yes, that was so yesterday, but just look what I can show him today! (*He pulls two pieces of paper halfway out of his breast pocket.*) The old woman needn't see. Here's two tickets to Peking. One for me and one for you. Do you still think your cousin's against the marriage?

SHEN TE. No. The job's good. And I don't have my store any more.

SUN. Because of you I sold our furniture.

SHEN TE. Don't go on! Don't show me the tickets! I'm too afraid I might simply go with you. But I can't give you the three hundred silver dollars, Sun. What's to become of the old couple?

SUN. And what's to become of me? (*pause*) Better drink some more! Or are you a cautious person? I don't want a cautious wife. If I drink, I'll fly again. And you, if you drink, you might possibly understand me.

SHEN TE. Don't think I don't understand you. You want to fly and I can't help you.

64

SUN. "Here's a plane, my darling, but it's only got one wing!"

SHEN TE. Sun, we can't get the job at Peking honestly. That's why I need the two hundred silver dollars which you got from me. Give them to me now, Sun!

SUN. "Give them to me now, Sun!" What exactly are you talking about? Are you my wife or aren't you? You're betraying me, you know that, don't you? Luckily for both of us, things don't depend on you. Everything's arranged.

MRS. YANG (*icily*). Sun, are you sure the bride's cousin is coming? Since he's still not here it might almost seem that he has something against this marriage.

SUN. What are you thinking of, Mamma? We're bosom friends! I'll open the door wide so he'll find us right away when he comes to be his friend Sun's best man. (*He goes to the door and kicks it open. Then he returns, staggering somewhat since he has already drunk too much, and sits down again beside Shen Te.*) We're waiting. Your cousin's got more sense than you. Love, he says wisely, goes with living! And, more important than that, he knows what it means to you: no more store and no marriage either!

(*Everyone is waiting.*)

MRS. YANG. Now!

(*Steps can be heard and everyone looks toward the door. But the steps pass.*)

MRS. SHIN. It's going to be a scandal. I can feel it. I can smell it. The bride is waiting for the wedding but the groom's waiting for her cousin.

SUN. The cousin's taking his time.

SHEN TE (*softly*). Oh, Sun!

SUN. To sit here with the tickets in my pocket and next to me a fool who doesn't know arithmetic. I can foresee the day when you'll send the police to my house to get the two hundred silver dollars.

SHEN TE (*to the audience*). He is bad and he wants me to be bad too. Here I am, I love him, and he waits for the cousin. But around me are the frail: the old woman with her sick husband, the poor who in the morning wait for their rice at my door, and an unknown man from Peking who is worried about his job. And they all protect me by trusting me.

SUN (*staring at the glass pitcher in which there is no wine left*). The glass pitcher of wine is our clock. We're poor people and when the guests have drunk the wine, the clock's run down forever.

(*Mrs. Yang beckons him to be silent, for steps can again be heard.*)

THE WAITER (*entering*). Do you want another pitcher of wine, Mrs. Yang?

MRS. YANG. No, I think we've got enough. Wine only makes you warm, doesn't it?

MRS. SHIN. It's expensive too, I'd say.

MRS. YANG. Drinking always makes me perspire.

THE WAITER. Might I ask, then, for a settlement of the bill?

MRS. YANG (*not hearing him*). Ladies and gentlemen, I ask you to be patient a little longer, the cousin *must* be on his way. (*To the Waiter*) Don't spoil the festivities!

THE WAITER. I can't let you leave without settling the bill.

MRS. YANG. But I'm known here!

THE WAITER. Exactly.

MRS. YANG. It's outrageous, the service today. What d'you say to that, Sun?

THE PRIEST. I take my leave. (*He goes off, ponderously.*)

MRS. YANG (*desperately*). Just stay where you are! The priest's coming back in a few minutes.

SUN. Never mind, Mamma. Ladies and gentlemen, since the priest's gone away, we can't keep you.

THE SISTER-IN-LAW. Come on, grandfather!

THE GRANDFATHER (*earnestly emptying his glass*). To the bride!

THE NIECE (*to Shen Te*). Don't hold it against him. He wants to be friendly. He likes you.

MRS. SHIN. What a disgrace!

(*All the guests go off.*)

SHEN TE. Shall I go too, Sun?

SUN. No, you'll wait. (*He drags her by her bridal ornaments, messing them up.*) Isn't it your wedding? I'm still waiting and the old woman's waiting too. *She* wants to see her falcon (*he points at himself*) in the clouds! However, I almost believe now that it'll be Saint Nevernever Day before she'll step to her door and see his plane thundering over her house. (*To the empty seats, as if the guests were still present*) Ladies and gentlemen, what's the matter with the conversation? Don't you like it here? The wedding, after all, is only postponed a bit because of the important guest who's expected and because the bride doesn't yet know the meaning of love. For your entertainment, I, the bridegroom, will sing you a song. (*He sings.*)

THE SONG OF SAINT NEVERNEVER DAY

On a certain day, as is very well known,
Everyone will cry "Hooray,
The poor woman's son is on the golden throne!"
And the day's Saint Nevernever Day.
On Saint Nevernever Day
He'll sit on the golden throne.

And on that day goodness will pay
And badness will cost you your head
And merit and gain will smile and play
While exchanging salt and bread.
On Saint Nevernever Day
While exchanging salt and bread.

And the grass will look down at the sky
And the pebbles will roll up the stream
And men will be good without batting an eye
They will make of our earth a dream.
On Saint Nevernever Day
They will make of our earth a dream.

And on that day I shall be a flier
And you'll be one of the best
And you, idle man, will have work at last

67

You, woman, will get your rest.
On Saint Nevernever Day
You, woman, will get your rest.

And because we can hardly wait for that time
All this will begin, I know,
Not at night, at seven or eight or nine,
But at the first cock crow.
On Saint Nevernever Day
At the very first cock crow.

MRS. YANG. He won't come now.
(*The three sit there, two of them looking toward the door.*)

6·A

Wang's sleeping quarters. Again the Gods appear to Wang in a dream. He has fallen asleep over a large book. Music.

WANG. I'm glad you've come, illustrious ones! Permit me a question which disturbs me deeply. In the ruined hut of a priest who has moved away to become a laborer in the cement factory, I found a book and in it a strange passage. I absolutely must read it to you. Here it is. (*With his left hand he turns the pages of an imaginary book above the real book which is lying in his lap. He lifts up the imaginary book to read from while the real book remains where it is.*) "In Sung there is a place called Thorngrove. Catalpas, cypresses, and mulberry trees grow there. Now trees which are one or two spans in circumference are cut down by those who want sticks to make dog kennels with. Those of three or four feet in circumference are cut down by rich families in search of boards for coffins. Those of seven or eight feet in circumference are cut down by people seeking beams for their luxury villas. Thus none of the trees lives its allotted span, for all perish before their time is up by saw and ax. Such are the tribulations of usefulness."

THE THIRD GOD. In that case the one men have least use for would be the best.

WANG. No, only the happiest. It's the worst but also the happiest.

THE FIRST GOD. The things people write!

THE SECOND GOD. Why does this parable affect you so deeply, water seller?

WANG. Because of Shen Te, illustrious one! She has come to grief in her love because she followed the commandment, love thy neighbor! Perhaps she is really *too* good for this world, illustrious ones!

THE FIRST GOD. Nonsense, weak and wretched man! Lice and doubts, it seems, have almost eaten you up.

WANG. Certainly, illustrious one, forgive me! I only thought you might be able to intervene.

THE FIRST GOD. That's quite impossible. Our friend here (*he points to the Third God who has a black eye*) intervened in a quarrel only yesterday. You can see the consequences.

WANG. But her cousin had to be called in again. He's an incredibly skillful man, as I found out for myself, but not even he could achieve anything. The store seems to be lost.

THE THIRD GOD (*a bit worried*). Perhaps we should help after all?

THE FIRST GOD. I'm of the opinion that she should help herself.

THE SECOND GOD (*sternly*). The worse the situation of a good man, the better he shows himself. Suffering ennobles!

THE FIRST GOD. All our hopes rest on her.

THE THIRD GOD. Things aren't what they might be with our search. Now and then we find some good beginnings, gratifying intentions, many high principles, but all that hardly constitutes a good human being. And when we do find halfway good people, they don't live in a dignified, human way. (*Confidentially*) Things are especially bad with our sleeping quarters. You can see where we spend the nights by the straw sticking to our clothes.

WANG. Just one thing, couldn't you at least . . .

THE GODS. No. We're onlookers. We firmly believe that our good woman will find her own way on this dark earth. The heavier the burden the greater will be her strength! Just wait, water seller, and, you'll see, everything will come to a good . . .

(*The figures of the Gods have grown paler, their voices softer, all the time. Now they disappear and their voices are no longer heard.*)

7

The yard behind Shen Te's tobacco store. On a cart there are a few house furnishings. Shen Te and Mrs. Shin are taking down the washing from the line.

MRS. SHIN. I can't understand why you don't fight for your store tooth and nail.

SHEN TE. What? I can't even pay the rent. The old couple's two hundred silver dollars have to be returned today but since I've given them to someone else, I'll have to sell my tobacco to Mrs. Mi Tzu.

MRS. SHIN. Everything's gone then. No husband, no tobacco, no place to stay! That's what happens when somebody wants to be better than other people. What are you going to live off now?

SHEN TE. I don't know. Perhaps I can earn a little by sorting tobacco.

MRS. SHIN. What are Mr. Shui Ta's pants doing here? He must have gone away from here naked!

SHEN TE. He's got another pair of trousers.

MRS. SHIN. I thought you said he'd gone for good? Why did he leave his pants behind?

SHEN TE. Perhaps he doesn't need them any more.

MRS. SHIN. Shall I pack them away?

SHEN TE. No.

(*Mr. Shu Fu comes running in.*)

MR. SHU FU. Don't say anything. I know all. You sacrificed your love and happiness so as not to ruin two old people who trusted you. It's not in vain that this neighborhood, this suspicious and malevolent neighborhood, calls you the Angel of the Suburbs. Your fiancé couldn't rise to your moral level, so you left him. And now you're closing your store, this little haven for so many! I can't let that pass. Morning after morning I watched from my doorstep the little crowd of wretched people in front of your store and you distributing rice with your own hands. Will that never happen again? Must the good woman of Setzuan perish? Oh, if only you'd permit me to assist you with your good works! No, don't say anything! I don't want any assurances. No avowals that you wish to accept my help! But here. (*He pulls out a checkbook and signs a check which he puts on her cart.*) I'm making out a blank check to you. You can fill it out as you wish, for any sum. And now I go, quietly and modestly, making no claims, on tiptoe, full of veneration, selflessly. (*Exit.*)

MRS. SHIN (*examining the check*). You're saved! The likes of you are lucky: you always find some idiot. But now fall to! Fill it out for a thousand silver dollars and I'll take it to the bank before he comes to his senses.

SHEN TE. Put the washing basket on the cart. I can pay the laundry bill without the check.

MRS. SHIN. What? You don't want to take the check? It's a crime! Is it just because you think you'd have to marry him? Sheer madness! People like him *want* to be led by the nose! It's the greatest bliss they know. Or do you still want to hold

on to your flier when Yellow Street and the whole neighborhood know how badly he treated you?

SHEN TE. It all comes from poverty. (*To the audience*)

> I saw him puff up his cheeks in his sleep. They
>   were bad cheeks.
> But in the morning I held his coat against the light
>   and saw the walls through it.
> When I heard his cunning laugh, I grew afraid.
> But when I saw his shoes full of holes, I loved
>   him dearly.

MRS. SHIN. So you're defending him after everything that's happened. I've never seen anyone quite as crazy. (*Angrily*) I
shall breathe more easily when we're rid of you in this neighborhood.

SHEN TE (*staggering while taking down the wash*). I'm a bit
dizzy.

MRS. SHIN (*taking the wash from her*). Do you often get dizzy
when you stretch or bend? If only there isn't a little visitor
on the way! (*She laughs.*) What a pretty mess! If that's
what's happened, it's all up with the big check! It wasn't
meant for an occasion of that sort.

(*She goes to the back with a basket. Shen Te looks after her
without moving. Then she looks at her body, feels it, and a
great joy comes over her face.*)

SHEN TE (*softly*). O joy! A human being is growing in my
womb. Nothing can be seen yet. But he's there already. The
world awaits him secretly. In the towns, people are saying:
Someone's coming now who's got to be reckoned with. (*In
pantomime she introduces her little son to the audience.*) A
flier!

> Welcome a new conqueror of unknown mountains and
>   unreachable regions!
> One who brings the mail from man to man over the
>   unpassable deserts!

(*She begins to walk up and down, leading her little son by
the hand.*) Come, son, look at the world! Here, that's a

72

tree. Bow to it, greet it. (*She shows him how to bow.*) That's it: now you know each other. Stop, here comes the water seller. A friend. Give him your hand. Don't be afraid. A glass of fresh water for my son, please. It's warm today. (*She gives him the glass.*) O dear, the policeman! We'll make a big circle around him. Perhaps we'll get a few cherries over there in the rich Mr. Feh Pung's garden. But we mustn't be seen there. Come, fatherless boy! You too want cherries! Easy, easy, son! (*They walk carefully, looking around.*) No, over here, the bushes will hide us. No, you can't go straight at them like that. (*He seems to pull her away. She resists.*) We've got to be reasonable. (*Suddenly she gives in.*) All right, if you really must go straight at them . . . (*She lifts him up.*) Can you reach the cherries? Push them in your mouth, that's a safe place for them. (*She takes a cherry from him and puts it in her mouth.*) Tastes pretty good. O heavens, the policeman! Now we've got to run! (*They flee.*) There's the street. Quiet now, we'll walk slowly so we won't be noticed. As if not the least thing had happened. (*She sings, walking along with the child.*)

> For no reason a plum
> Attacked a bum.
> But the man, very quick,
> Bit the plum in the neck.

(*Wang, the water seller, has come in, leading a child by the hand. He watches Shen Te with wonder. Wang coughs.*)

SHEN TE. Oh, Wang! Hello.

WANG. Shen Te, I've heard you're not so well off. You even had to sell your store to pay your debts. But here's a child without a roof over his head. He was running about in the stockyards. He seems to be one of Lin To's children. You remember the carpenter? He lost his shop a few weeks ago and has been drinking ever since. His children go hungry and hang around the streets. What can be done for them?

SHEN TE (*taking the child from him*). Come, little man! (*To the audience*)

73

You there! Someone is asking for shelter.
A bit of tomorrow is asking for a today!
His friend, the conqueror, whom you know,
Is his advocate.

(*To Wang*) He can easily live in Mr. Shu Fu's cabins where I also may be going. I'm to have a baby too. But don't tell anyone or Yang Sun will hear it, and we'd only be in his way. Look for Mr. Lin To downtown, and tell him to come here.

WANG. Thanks a lot, Shen Te. I knew you'd find something. (*To the child*) You see, someone who's *good* always knows a way out. I'll run quickly and get your father. (*He starts to go.*)

SHEN TE. Oh Wang, now it comes back to me: how's your hand? I *wanted* to take the oath for you but my cousin . . .

WANG. Don't worry about my hand. Look, I've already learned to get along without my right hand. I hardly need it any more. (*He shows her how he can handle his pole without using his right hand.*) Watch how I do it!

SHEN TE. But it mustn't grow stiff! There, take the cart, sell everything, and go to the doctor with the money. I'm ashamed to have let you down like this. And what will you think of my accepting the cabins from the barber?

WANG. The homeless can live there now. And so can you. That's more important than my hand. Now I'm going to get the carpenter. (*Exit.*)

SHEN TE. Promise me you'll go to the doctor!

(*Mrs. Shin has returned and has been waving to her.*)

MRS. SHIN. Are you crazy? Giving away the cart with your very last possessions! What's his hand to you? If the barber hears of it, he'll chase you out of the only shelter you can get. You haven't paid me for the laundry!

SHEN TE. Why are you so bad?

You tread on your fellow man.
Isn't it a strain?
Your veins swell with your efforts to be greedy.
Extended naturally, a hand gives and receives
    with equal ease.

74

Grabbing greedily, it has to strain. Alas!
What an enticement, to give! How pleasant,
    to be kind!
A good word slips out like a sigh of contentment.

(*Mrs. Shin goes angrily off.*)

SHEN TE (*to the child*). Sit down here and wait till your father comes.

(*The child sits on the ground. Enter the Husband and Wife who came to live with Shen Te on the day her store opened. They are dragging large sacks.*)

THE WIFE. Are you alone, Shen Te? (*Since Shen Te nods, she calls in her Nephew who is also carrying a sack.*) Where's your cousin?

SHEN TE. He's gone away.

THE WIFE. And is he coming back?

SHEN TE. No. I'm giving up the store.

THE WIFE. We know that. That's why we came. We've got a few sacks of raw tobacco here which someone owed us and we'd like to ask you to move them to your new home together with your belongings. We haven't got a place yet to take them to and we'd be so noticeable on the street. I don't see how you can deny us this small favor after all the trouble we got into in your store.

SHEN TE. I'll gladly do you the favor.

THE HUSBAND. And if someone should ask whose sacks these are, you can say they're yours.

SHEN TE. Who should ask me?

THE WIFE (*looking at her sharply*). The police, for instance. They are prejudiced against us and want to ruin us. Where should we put the sacks?

SHEN TE. I don't know, just now I'd rather not do anything that might get me in jail.

THE WIFE. That's just like you. We're to lose the few miserable sacks of tobacco too, the only things we saved!

(*Shen Te maintains a stubborn silence.*)

THE HUSBAND. Just think, this tobacco could start us in the manufacturing business. We could go a long way!

75

SHEN TE. All right, I'll keep the sacks for you. For the time being, we'll put them in the back room.

(*She goes in with them. The child looks after her. Then, shyly glancing about, he goes to the garbage can and fishes around in it. He starts to eat out of it. Shen Te and the others come back.*)

THE WIFE. You understand, I guess, that we depend on you completely.

SHEN TE. Yes. (*She sees the child and grows rigid.*)

THE HUSBAND. We'll look for you the day after tomorrow in Mr. Shu Fu's cabins.

SHEN TE. Go now, quickly. I'm not well.

(*She pushes them off. Exeunt the three.*)

SHEN TE. He is hungry. He's fishing in the garbage can. (*She picks up the child and, in the following speech, expresses her horror at the fate of poor children. She shows the audience the little gray mouth. She asserts her determination under no circumstances to treat her own child with such cruelty. During her speech the musicians start playing "The Song of the Defenselessness of the Gods and Good Men."*)

O son! O flier! Into what a world will you come?
They want to let you fish in the garbage can, even you!
Only look at the little gray mouth!
(*She shows the child to the audience.*)
How do you treat your offspring?
Have you no mercy on the fruit of your womb?
No pity for yourselves, unhappy men?
I shall defend my own even if I have to be a tigress
  to do it!
Having seen this, from now on, I divorce myself
  from everybody!
I will not rest till I have saved my son, if only him!
What I have learned in my school, the gutter,
With fisticuffs and deceit,
Will now be of use to you, my son!
I will be good to you, and a tigress, a wild beast
To all others,

76

If I have to.
And I *shall* have to.

(*She goes off to change into the cousin's clothes.*)

SHEN TE (*going*). Once more it has to be. The last time, I hope. (*She has taken with her Shui Ta's trousers. The returning Mrs. Shin looks after her curiously. Enter the Sister-in-law and the Grandfather. The music continues softly.*)

THE SISTER-IN-LAW. The store's closed. The furniture's in the yard. That's the end.

MRS. SHIN. The results of frivolity, sensuality, and self-love. And where's the journey to? Down, down, down! Into Mr. Shu Fu's cabins. With you.

THE SISTER-IN-LAW. She'll have a nice surprise! We've come to complain! Damp rat holes with rotten floors! The barber only offered them to us because his soap supplies got moldy there. "I have shelter for you, what do you say to that?" Shame! we say to that!

(*Enter the Unemployed.*)

THE UNEMPLOYED. Is it true, Shen Te's moving away?

THE SISTER-IN-LAW. Yes, she wanted to sneak off. No one was supposed to find out.

MRS. SHIN. She's ashamed because she's ruined.

THE UNEMPLOYED (*excitedly*). She's got to call her cousin! Advise her to call her cousin! He's the only one who can still do something.

THE SISTER-IN-LAW. That's true. He's stingy enough but at least he'll save her store and then she'll help us again.

THE UNEMPLOYED. I wasn't thinking of us, I was thinking of her. But, you're right, she should call him for our sake too.

(*Enter Wang with the Carpenter. He leads two children by the hand.*)

THE CARPENTER. I really can't thank you enough. (*To the others*) We're getting a place to live.

MRS. SHIN. Where?

THE CARPENTER. Mr. Shu Fu's cabins! And it was little Feng who brought the change about! (*He sees Feng.*) Well, here you are! "Here is someone asking for shelter," Miss Shen Te

77

is supposed to have said, and at once she got us a place to stay. (*To the two children*) Thank your brother, you two! (*The Carpenter and his children gaily bow to the child.*) Our thanks, little friend!

(*Shui Ta has entered.*)

SHUI TA. May I ask what you all want here?

THE UNEMPLOYED. Mr. Shui Ta!

WANG. Good day, Mr. Shui Ta. I didn't know you'd come back. You know the carpenter, Mr. Lin To. Miss Shen Te has promised him a place in Mr. Shu Fu's cabins.

SHUI TA. Mr. Shu Fu's cabins are not available.

THE CARPENTER. So we can't live there?

SHUI TA. The space is reserved for something else.

THE SISTER-IN-LAW. Does that mean *we* have to get out too?

SHUI TA. I'm afraid so.

THE SISTER-IN-LAW. But where are we all to go?

SHUI TA (*shrugging his shoulders*). As I understand Miss Shen Te, who has gone on a journey, it is not her intention to withdraw her aid completely. However, in the future, things will be ordered a bit more reasonably. No more food without services rendered in return. Instead, everyone will be given the opportunity to work himself up in an honest way. Miss Shen Te has decided to give you all work. Those of you who want to follow me now into Shu Fu's cabins will not be led into nothingness.

THE SISTER-IN-LAW. Does that mean we're all supposed to work for Shen Te now?

SHUI TA. Yes. You'll be making tobacco. In the room inside are three bales of goods. Get them!

THE SISTER-IN-LAW. Don't forget we owned a store once. We prefer to work for ourselves. We have our own tobacco.

SHUI TA (*to the Unemployed and the Carpenter*). Perhaps *you* will want to work for Shen Te since you don't have your own tobacco.

(*The Carpenter and the Unemployed go in dejectedly. The Landlady enters.*)

THE LANDLADY. Well, Mr. Shui Ta, how're things with the sale? Here I have three hundred silver dollars.

SHUI TA. Mrs. Mi Tzu, I've decided not to sell, but to sign the lease.

THE LANDLADY. What? All of a sudden you don't need the money for the flier?

SHUI TA. No.

THE LANDLADY. And do you have the rent?

SHUI TA (*taking the barber's check from the cart and filling it out*). Here I have a check for ten thousand silver dollars, made out by Mr. Shu Fu, who's interested in my cousin. Mrs. Mi Tzu, look for yourself. The two hundred silver dollars for the next half year's rent will be in your hands before 6 P.M. And now, Mrs. Mi Tzu, allow me to continue my work. I'm very busy today and have to ask your pardon.

THE LANDLADY. Oh I see, Mr. Shu Fu steps into the flier's shoes! Ten thousand silver dollars! Nevertheless, Mr. Shui Ta, the young girls of today surprise me. They are fickle. And superficial too.

(*She goes out. The Carpenter and the Unemployed drag in the sacks.*)

THE CARPENTER. I don't know why I'm dragging your sacks.

SHUI TA. It's enough that I know. Your son here has a healthy appetite. He wants to eat, Mr. Lin To.

THE SISTER-IN-LAW (*seeing the sacks*). Has my brother-in-law been here?

MRS. SHIN. Yes.

THE SISTER-IN-LAW. I thought so. I know these sacks. That's our tobacco!

SHUI TA. You better not say that so loud. This is my tobacco, as you can see from the fact that it was standing in my room. If you have any doubts, we can go to the police and remove them. Is that what you want?

THE SISTER-IN-LAW (*angrily*). No.

SHUI TA. It seems you don't have tobacco of your own after all. Under these circumstances you will perhaps grasp the saving hand which Miss Shen Te is holding out to you? Be so kind now as to show me the way to Mr. Shu Fu's cabins.

(*Taking the Carpenter's youngest child by the hand, Shui Ta goes off, followed by the Carpenter, his other children, the*

Sister-in-law, the Grandfather, and the Unemployed. The Sister-in-law, the Carpenter, and the Unemployed drag the sacks.)

WANG. He's a bad man. But Shen Te is good.

MRS. SHIN. I don't know. A pair of pants is missing from the clothes line and her cousin's wearing them. That must mean something. I'd like to know what.

(Enter the old couple.)

THE OLD WOMAN. Isn't Miss Shen Te here?

MRS. SHIN *(absent-mindedly)*. Gone away.

THE OLD WOMAN. That's strange. She was going to bring us something.

WANG *(sadly looking at his hand)*. She was going to help me too. My hand's getting all stiff. I'm sure she'll be back soon. The cousin has never stayed long.

MRS. SHIN. He hasn't, has he?

7·A

Wang's sleeping quarters. Music. In his dream, the water seller tells the Gods his fears. The Gods are still on their long journey. They seem tired. Stopping for a moment, they look over their shoulders toward the water seller.

WANG. Before your sudden appearance woke me, illustrious ones, I was dreaming. I saw my dear sister Shen Te in great distress in the rushes by the river at the place where those who commit suicide are found. She was staggering strangely and held her head low as if she were dragging something soft but heavy which was pulling her down in the mud. When

I called to her, she told me she had to take the package of rules to the other shore without getting it wet since that would wipe away the writing. Actually I couldn't see that she was carrying anything. But I remembered with fear that you, the gods, had spoken to her about the great virtues, in gratitude for her taking you in when you were hard put to it for sleeping quarters, O shame! I'm sure you'll understand my worries.

THE THIRD GOD. What do you propose?

WANG. Somewhat fewer rules, illustrious ones! A little relaxation of the book of rules, benevolent ones, in view of the bad times.

THE THIRD GOD. As for instance, Wang, as for instance?

WANG. As for instance that only good will be required, instead of love, or . . .

THE THIRD GOD. But that would be even more difficult, unhappy one!

WANG. Or fairness instead of justice.

THE THIRD GOD. But that would mean more work!

WANG. Then just propriety instead of honor.

THE THIRD GOD. But, don't you see, that would mean *more* work, not less, you skeptic! (*Tired, they wander on.*)

8

Shui Ta's tobacco factory. Shui Ta has established a small to- bacco factory in Mr. Shu Fu's cabins. Behind bars, fearfully close together, are several families, especially women and chil- dren. Among them are the Sister-in-law, the Grandfather, the Carpenter, and his children. Enter Mrs. Yang followed by Yang Sun.

81

MRS. YANG (*to the audience*). I have to tell you how the wisdom and strength of the universally respected Mr. Shui Ta has transformed my son Yang Sun from a depraved scamp into a useful person. As the whole neighborhood found out, Mr. Shui Ta opened a small but soon flourishing tobacco factory near the cattle runs. Three months ago I found it necessary to visit him there with my son. After a short time he received me.

(*Shui Ta comes out of the factory and goes to Mrs. Yang.*)

SHUI TA. How can I help you, Mrs. Yang?

MRS. YANG. Mr. Shui Ta, I'd like to put in a word for my son. This morning the police were at our house and we were told that you have brought an action in the name of Miss Shen Te for breach of promise of marriage. You also claim that Sun dishonestly got his hands on two hundred silver dollars.

SHUI TA. Quite right, Mrs. Yang.

MRS. YANG. Mr. Shui Ta, for the sake of the gods, couldn't you be merciful once more? The money's gone. He ran through it in two days when nothing came of the flying job. I know he's a good-for-nothing. He'd already sold my furniture and wanted to go to Peking without his old Mamma. (*She weeps.*) Miss Shen Te thought very highly of him once.

SHUI TA. What do you have to say, Mr. Yang Sun?

SUN (*darkly*). The money's gone.

SHUI TA. Mrs. Yang, because of my cousin's incomprehensible weakness for your depraved son, I'm prepared to give him another chance. She told me that she expected honest work to produce an improvement. He can have a job in my factory. We will deduct the two hundred silver dollars from his salary bit by bit.

SUN. Then it's the factory or the jail?

SHUI TA. Take your choice.

SUN. And I guess I can't talk with Shen Te?

SHUI TA. No.

SUN. Where's my place?

MRS. YANG. A thousand thanks, Mr. Shui Ta! You are infinitely kind. The gods will reward you. (*To Sun*) You've departed

82

from the right path. Now try your hand at honest work till you can face your mother again!

(*Sun follows Shui Ta into the factory. Mrs. Yang returns to the footlights.*)

MRS. YANG. The first weeks were hard for Sun. The work didn't agree with him. He had little opportunity to distinguish himself. But in the third week a small incident came to his aid. (*Sun and the former Carpenter Lin To are each dragging two bales of tobacco.*)

THE CARPENTER (*he stops, groaning, and sits down on a bale*). I can hardly go on. I'm not young enough for this work.

SUN (*sitting down too*). Why don't you just throw the sacks in their faces?

THE CARPENTER. And how're we to live? To get a bare living I've even got to use the children. If Miss Shen Te could see this! She was good.

SUN. She was all right. If conditions hadn't been so lousy, we could have made out quite nicely together. I'd like to know where she is. We better go on. *He* usually comes about this time.

(*They get up. Sun sees Shui Ta approaching.*)

SUN. Give me one of your sacks, you cripple! (*Sun takes one of the bales from Lin To.*)

THE CARPENTER. Thanks a lot! Now if *she* were here and saw how you help an old man you'd soon be in favor. Oh dear! (*Enter Shui Ta.*)

MRS. YANG. And of course Mr. Shui Ta saw right away what it means to be a good worker not shrinking from any job. And he stepped in.

SHUI TA. Stop, you! What's going on? Are you only carrying one sack?

THE CARPENTER. I'm a bit tired today, Mr. Shui Ta, and Yang Sun was kind enough to . . .

SHUI TA. You're going back to take three bales, my friend. What Yang Sun can do, you can do. Yang Sun has the right attitude and you have not.

MRS. YANG (*while the former Carpenter gets two more bales*).

Of course, not a word to Sun but Mr. Shui Ta was wise to the situation. And the following Saturday when the wages were being paid out . . .

(*A table is brought in and Shui Ta arrives with a bag of money. Standing next to the foreman — the former Unemployed — he pays the wages. Sun steps up to the table.*)

THE UNEMPLOYED. Yang Sun, six silver dollars.

SUN. Excuse me, it can't be more than five. Only five silver dollars. (*He takes the list held by the foreman.*) Please look, here are marked *six* working days. That's a mistake. I was absent one day because of some court business. (*Hypocritically*) I don't want to get anything I don't deserve, however lousy the pay is!

THE UNEMPLOYED. Okay, five silver dollars! (*To Shui Ta*) A rare case, Mr. Shui Ta!

SHUI TA. How can it say six days here if it was only five?

THE UNEMPLOYED. I must have made a mistake, Mr. Shui Ta. (*To Sun, coldly*) It won't happen again.

SHUI TA (*calling Sun aside*). I noticed the other day that you're a strong man and don't hold your strength back. You give it to the firm. Today I see you're even honest. Does it often happen that the foreman makes mistakes in favor of the employees?

SUN. He's got friends among the workers and they look on him as one of themselves.

SHUI TA. I see. Well, one good turn deserves another. Would you like some little recompense?

SUN. No. But perhaps I may point to the fact that I'm also intelligent. I've had an education, you know. The foreman means well enough by the workers but he's uneducated and can't understand what the firm needs. Give me a trial period of one week, Mr. Shui Ta, and I think I'll be able to prove to you that my intelligence can be worth more to the firm than my physical strength.

MRS. YANG. Those were daring words, but that evening I said to my son: You're a flier. Show that, even where you are now, you can rise! Fly, my falcon! And, really, education and intelligence can do great things! How can you belong to the better sort of people without them? My son worked true miracles in Mr. Shui Ta's factory!

(*Sun stands with his legs apart behind the workers. Above their heads is a basket of raw tobacco which they are handing along.*)

SUN. You there, I don't call that honest work! This basket has got to move faster! (*To a child*) Sit on the floor where you don't take up so much room! And you, yes you over there, you can easily take on the pressing too! Lazy dogs, what're you getting paid for? Hurry up with the basket! The devil! Put grandfather on one side and let him pick with the children! No more laziness now! To my beat, the whole thing! (*He claps the rhythm with his hands and the basket moves faster.*)

MRS. YANG. And no enmity, no abuse from uneducated people — and there was plenty of it — could stop my son from doing his duty.

(*One of the workers starts The Song of the Eighth Elephant. The others join in the refrain.*)

THE SONG OF THE EIGHTH ELEPHANT
Seven elephants had Mr. Dschin
And then there was Number Eight.
Seven were wild, Number Eight was tame
Number Eight guarded the gate.
Run faster!
Mr. Dschin has a forest park
It must be cleared before nightfall
And now it will soon be dark!

Seven elephants were clearing the forest
Mr. Dschin rode Number Eight.
And when the seven toiled all day
Number Eight would quietly wait.
Dig faster!
Mr. Dschin has a forest park

It must be cleared before nightfall
And now it will soon be dark!

Seven elephants had had enough
Of felling trees each day till late.
Mr. Dschin was angry at the seven, but he
Gave a bushel of rice to Number Eight.
What does it mean?
Mr. Dschin has a forest park
It must be cleared before nightfall
And now it will soon be dark!

Seven elephants they hadn't a tusk
Number Eight had a tusk which he used.
And when Number Eight cut the other seven up
Mr. Dschin stood there and was amused.
Keep on digging!
Mr. Dschin has a forest park
It must be cleared before nightfall
And now it will soon be dark!

(*Smoking a cigar, Shui Ta has come casually strolling forward. Yang Sun, laughing, has joined in the refrain of the third stanza and speeded up the tempo of the last by clapping his hands.*)

MRS. YANG. We really can't thank Mr. Shui Ta enough. Almost without lifting a finger, with wisdom and strength alone, he's brought out all the good that lay hidden in Sun. He didn't make him fantastic promises like his cousin whom they praise so highly. He just forced him into honest work. Today, Sun is quite a different person. You'll have to admit that! A noble man is like a bell. If you ring it, it rings, and if you don't, it don't, as the saying goes.

9

Shen Te's tobacco store. The store has become an office with club chairs and fine carpets. It is raining. Shui Ta, now fat, is sending away the Old Man and his wife. Mrs. Shin, amused, looks on. She is obviously in new clothes.

SHUI TA. I'm sorry I can't tell you when she'll be back.

THE OLD WOMAN. We got a letter today with the two hundred silver dollars which we once lent her. It had no return address. But the letter must have come from Shen Te. We'd like to write to her. What's her address?

SHUI TA. I'm sorry I don't know that either.

THE OLD MAN. Let's go.

THE OLD WOMAN. She's got to come back sometime.

(*Shui Ta bows. The two old people go off, uncertain and worried.*)

MRS. SHIN. They got their money too late. Now they've lost their store because they couldn't pay their taxes.

SHUI TA. Why didn't they come to me?

MRS. SHIN. People don't like to come to you. At first, I guess, they were waiting for Shen Te to come back, because they had nothing in writing. Then at the critical moment the old man got a fever and his wife stayed with him day and night.

SHUI TA (*he has to sit down; he is beginning to feel sick*). I'm dizzy again.

MRS. SHIN (*attending to him*). You're in your seventh month! The excitement isn't good for you. You can be glad you've got me. No one can get along without help from others. Well, I'll be at your side when your hardest hour comes. (*She laughs.*)

SHUI TA (*weakly*). Can I count on it, Mrs. Shin?

MRS. SHIN. I'll say. Of course it'll cost you a bit. Open your collar, you'll feel better.

SHUI TA (*wretchedly*). It's all for the child's sake, Mrs. Shin.

MRS. SHIN. All for the child.

87

SHUI TA. I'm getting fat too fast. It must draw attention.

MRS. SHIN. They put it down to your wealth.

SHUI TA. And what'll happen to the little one?

MRS. SHIN. You ask that three times a day. It'll be taken care of. It'll have the best that money can buy.

SHUI TA. Yes. (*anxiously*) And it must never see Shui Ta.

MRS. SHIN. Never. Always Shen Te.

SHUI TA. But the rumors in the neighborhood! The things the water seller says! The store is watched!

MRS. SHIN. As long as the barber doesn't know anything, nothing's lost. Drink some of this water.

(*Enter Sun in a smart suit and with a businessman's brief case. He looks surprised at finding Shui Ta in Mrs. Shin's arms.*)

SUN. I guess I'm intruding.

SHUI TA (*getting up with difficulty and going to the door, staggering*). Until tomorrow, Mrs. Shin!

(*Mrs. Shin, putting on her gloves, smiles and goes off.*)

SUN. Gloves! Where from, what for, and how? Is she fleecing you maybe? (*Since Shui Ta does not answer*) Are even you susceptible to the tender emotions? Funny. (*He takes a sheet of paper out of his brief case.*) Anyway, you haven't been at your best, lately, not as you used to be. Moods. Indecisions. Are you ill? The business suffers. Here's another letter from the police. They want to close the factory. They say that at the very most they can only permit twice the lawful number of workers. You've got to do something now, Mr. Shui Ta. (*Shui Ta looks at him absent-mindedly for a moment. Then he goes into the back room and returns with a bag. He pulls out a new bowler hat and throws it on the desk.*)

SHUI TA. The firm wishes its representatives to be decently dressed.

SUN. Did you buy that for me?

SHUI TA (*indifferently*). Try it on and see if it fits.

(*Sun is surprised but puts it on. Shui Ta looks him over and puts the bowler in place.*)

SUN. Your servant! But don't evade me again! You've got to discuss the new project with the barber today.

SHUI TA. The barber's demanding impossible conditions.

SUN. Of what kind? If only you'd tell me.

SHUI TA (*evasively*). The cabins are good enough.

SUN. Yes, good enough for the rabble working there. But not good enough for the tobacco. It gets damp. Before the meeting I'll have a talk with Mrs. Mi Tzu about *her* buildings. If we have them, we can fire this bunch of beggars, abortions, and walking scarecrows. They're not good enough. We'll have a cup of tea, I'll stroke Mrs. Mi Tzu's fat knees, and we'll get her buildings half price.

SHUI TA (*sharply*). No. In the interest of the firm's reputation, I want your behavior always to be personally reserved and coolly businesslike.

SUN. Why are you so irritated? Are those unpleasant rumors bothering you?

SHUI TA. I don't pay any attention to rumors.

SUN. Then it must be the rain again. Rain always makes you irritable and melancholy. I'd like to know why.

WANG'S VOICE (*from outside*).

> I'm selling water, water,
> As I stand here in the rain.
> For such a little water
> I've suffered too much pain.
> And now I shout: "Buy water!"
> But no one's buying
> Parched and dying
> And drinking and paying . . .

SUN. Here's that damned water seller. He'll be starting his heckling again.

WANG'S VOICE (*from outside*). Aren't there any good people left in the city of Setzuan? Not even here on the square where the good Shen Te used to live? Where is she who even when it was raining bought a little water from me in the gladness of her heart many months ago? Where is she now? Has no one seen her? Has no one heard from her? She went into this house one evening and never came out again.

SUN. Shall I shut his trap for him? What's it to him where she is? By the way, I think you're only keeping it secret so that *I* won't find out.

WANG (*entering*). Mr. Shui Ta, I'm asking you again when Shen Te will come back. It's six months now since she went away. (*Shui Ta is silent.*) In the meantime much has happened which she would never have put up with. (*Shui Ta is still silent.*) Mr. Shui Ta, there are rumors in the district that something must have happened to Shen Te. We, her friends, are very worried. Have the goodness to give us her address!

SHUI TA. Unfortunately, I'm not free at the moment, Mr. Wang. Come back next week.

WANG (*excitedly*). In the mornings there used to be rice at her door. For the needy. It has been there again lately!

SHUI TA. And what do people conclude from this?

WANG. That Shen Te hasn't gone away at all, but . . .

SHUI TA. But what? (*Wang is silent.*) Then I'll give you my answer. And it is final. If you're Shen Te's friend, Mr. Wang, ask about her as little as possible. That's my advice.

WANG. Nice advice! Mr. Shui Ta, Shen Te told me before her disappearance that she was pregnant!

SUN. What?

SHUI TA (*quickly*). It's a lie!

WANG (*very earnestly to Shui Ta*). Mr. Shui Ta, you mustn't believe that Shen Te's friends will stop asking about her. A good person isn't so easily forgotten. There aren't many. (*Exit.*)

(*Motionless, Shui Ta looks after him, then goes quickly into the back room.*)

SUN (*to the audience*). Shen Te pregnant! I'm beside myself! I've been swindled! She must have told her cousin right away and that scoundrel sent her away immediately! "Pack your suitcase and disappear before the child's father gets wind of it." It's absolutely unnatural. It's inhuman. I have a son, a Yang appears on the scene, and what happens? The girl disappears and I'm left here to slave! (*He gets angry.*) I'm put off with a hat! (*He stamps on it.*) Criminal! Thief! Kidnapper! And the girl's virtually without a protector!

(*Sobbing can be heard from the back room. He stands still.*)
Did I hear sobbing? Who is it? It's stopped. What sobs are
these? That cunning dog Shui Ta doesn't sob! Who sobs
then? And what does it mean that the rice is said to be at the
door in the mornings? Is the girl here after all? Is he just
hiding her? Who else could be sobbing? That would be just
the thing I want! If she's pregnant I've got to find her!
(*Shui Ta returns from the back room. He goes to the door
and looks out into the rain.*)

SUN. Well, where is she?

SHUI TA (*putting up his hand and listening*). Just a moment!
It's nine o'clock. But one can't hear a thing today. The rain's
too heavy.

SUN (*ironically*). And what do you want to hear?

SHUI TA. The mail plane.

SUN. Stop fooling.

SHUI TA. I was once told that you wanted to fly? Have you lost
that desire?

SUN. I'm not complaining about my present position, if that's
what you mean. I don't care for night work, you know. Flying the mail is night work. The firm's become very dear to
me, so to speak. It is after all the firm of my one-time future
wife, even if she has gone away. And she has, hasn't she?

SHUI TA. Why do you ask?

SUN. Maybe because her affairs still don't leave me altogether
unmoved.

SHUI TA. That might interest my cousin.

SUN. In any case, I'm still sufficiently concerned in her affairs
not to close my eyes if, for instance, she were kept under
lock and key.

SHUI TA. By whom?

SUN. By you!
(*Pause*)

SHUI TA. What would you do?

SUN. I might, to begin with, start arguing about my position in
the firm.

SHUI TA. Oh, I see. And if the firm, that is, if *I* should give you

91

an adequate position, could I count on your giving up all further investigations concerning your one-time future wife?

SUN. Perhaps.

SHUI TA. And what sort of new position are you thinking of?

SUN. The top one. I'd be thinking of throwing you out, for example.

SHUI TA. And if, instead of me, the firm threw *you* out?

SUN. I'd probably come back. And not alone.

SHUI TA. But?

SUN. With the police.

SHUI TA. With the police. And suppose the police found no one here?

SUN. Then I suppose they'd search this back room. Mr. Shui Ta, my longing for the lady of my heart is insatiable. I feel I must do something in order to fold her in my arms again. (*Calmly*) She's pregnant and needs someone around. I've got to talk it over with the water seller. (*He goes.*)

(*Shui Ta looks after him without moving. Then he quickly returns to the back room. He brings out various belongings of Shen Te's, underwear, dresses, toilet articles. He looks a long time at the shawl which Shen Te bought from the Old Man and his wife. He then makes all these things up into a bundle and, hearing a noise, hides it under the table. Enter the Landlady and Mr. Shu Fu. They greet Shui Ta and put away their umbrellas and rubbers.*)

THE LANDLADY. Fall's coming on, Mr. Shui Ta.

MR. SHU FU. A sad season!

THE LANDLADY. And where's your charming secretary? A terrible lady-killer! But I guess you don't know that side of him. All the same he knows how to combine charm with attention to business in a way which can only be to your advantage.

SHUI TA (*bowing*). Won't you take a seat?

(*They sit down and start smoking.*)

SHUI TA. My friends, an unforeseen incident which might have certain consequences forces me to speed up the negotiations. Negotiations concerning the future of the project I've been working on. Mr. Shu Fu, my factory is in difficulties.

MR. SHU FU. It always is.

SHUI TA. But now the police are openly threatening to close it if I can't point to negotiations for a new project. Mr. Shu Fu, it's a question of my cousin's one piece of property. Now you've always displayed the liveliest interest in my cousin.

MR. SHU FU. Mr. Shui Ta, I have a deep aversion to talking about your constantly expanding projects. I speak about a small dinner with your cousin; you hint at financial difficulties. I put cabins for the homeless at your cousin's disposal; you establish a factory there. I hand her a check; you present it. Your cousin disappears; you ask for ten thousand silver dollars, remarking that my cabins are too small. Sir, where *is* your cousin?

SHUI TA. Mr. Shu Fu, don't worry. I can inform you today that she'll be back very soon.

MR. SHU FU. Soon? When? You've been saying "soon" for weeks.

SHUI TA. I'm not demanding new signatures from you. I've merely asked whether you'd show more interest in my project if my cousin returned.

MR. SHU FU. I've told you a thousand times that I'm ready to discuss everything with your cousin and nothing with you. However, it seems that you want to put obstacles in the way of such a discussion.

SHUI TA. Not any more.

MR. SHU FU. When will it take place then?

SHUI TA (*uncertainly*). In three months.

MR. SHU FU (*annoyed*). Then I'll sign in three months.

SHUI TA. But everything has to be prepared.

MR. SHU FU. You can prepare everything, Shui Ta, if you're convinced that your cousin will really come at this time.

SHUI TA. Mrs. Mi Tzu, are you, for your part, ready to confirm to the police that I may have your workrooms?

THE LANDLADY. Certainly, if you'll let me have your secretary. You've known for weeks that's my condition. (*To Mr. Shu Fu*) The young man's so efficient in business and I need a manager.

93

SHUI TA. You've got to understand that I can't do without Mr. Yang Sun just now, with all the difficulties I'm having. And my health has been failing me lately. I was ready from the beginning to let you have him, but . . .

THE LANDLADY. Yes, but?

(*Pause*)

SHUI TA. All right, he'll call on you tomorrow, in your office.

MR. SHU FU. I am very glad that you were able to reach this decision, Shui Ta. Should Miss Shen Te really come back, the young man's presence would be highly improper. As we know, he once exerted a most harmful influence over her.

SHUI TA (*bowing*). Doubtless. Please excuse my long hesitation over the question of my cousin Shen Te and Mr. Yang Sun. It is not worthy of a businessman. But they were once very close to each other.

THE LANDLADY. You're excused.

SHUI TA (*looking toward the door*). My friends, let us now reach a settlement. In this once small and shabby store where the poor people of the neighborhood bought the good Shen Te's tobacco, we, her friends, are resolving to establish twelve beautiful new stores which in the future will sell Shen Te's good tobacco. I'm told people are calling me the Tobacco King of Setzuan. Actually I carried on this business solely in my cousin's interests. It will belong to her, her children, and her grandchildren.

(*The noise of a crowd can be heard from outside. Enter Sun, Wang, and the Policeman.*)

THE POLICEMAN. Mr. Shui Ta, I'm very sorry the excited state of this neighborhood forces me to follow up a report originating in your own firm. According to this report you are depriving your cousin Miss Shen Te of her freedom.

SHUI TA. It's not true.

THE POLICEMAN. Mr. Yang Sun here testifies that from the room behind your office he heard sobbing which could only come from a female.

THE LANDLADY. That's ridiculous. I and Mr. Shu Fu, two respected citizens of this city whose evidence could hardly be doubted by the police, can testify that no one has been sobbing here. We are quietly smoking our cigars.

THE POLICEMAN. Unfortunately I have orders to inspect the room in question.

(*Shui Ta opens the door. The Policeman bows and steps into the doorway. He looks into the room, then turns round and smiles.*)

THE POLICEMAN. There's really nobody in there.

SUN (*who has been following him*). But I heard sobbing! (*His eye lights on the table under which Shui Ta has pushed the bundle. He spots the bundle.*) That wasn't here before! (*Opening it, he shows Shen Te's dresses and other things.*)

WANG. Those are Shen Te's things! (*He runs to the door and calls out.*) Her clothes have been discovered here!

THE POLICEMAN (*taking the things*). You declare that your cousin's gone away. A bundle with things of hers is found hidden under your table. Where can the girl be reached, Mr. Shui Ta?

SHUI TA. I don't know her address.

THE POLICEMAN. That is most regrettable.

SHOUTS FROM THE CROWD. Shen Te's things have been found! The Tobacco King has murdered the girl and put her out of the way!

THE POLICEMAN. Mr. Shui Ta, I shall have to ask you to follow me to the station.

SHUI TA (*bowing to the Landlady and Mr. Shu Fu*). I have to apologize for this scandal, my friends. But there are still judges in Setzuan. I'm convinced that everything will shortly be cleared up. (*He goes out, the Policeman at his back.*)

WANG. A terrible crime has been committed!

SUN (*dismayed*). But I heard sobbing!

Wang's sleeping quarters. Music. For the last time the Gods appear to the water seller in his dream. They have changed considerably. There are unmistakable signs of a long journey, extreme exhaustion, and manifold unhappy experiences. One has had his hat struck off his head, one has lost a leg in a fox trap, and all three go barefoot.

WANG. At last you've come! Terrible things have been happening in Shen Te's tobacco store, illustrious ones. Shen Te went away again many months ago! Her cousin seized everything! Today he's been arrested. He's supposed to have murdered her to get her store. But I don't believe it. I had a dream in which she came and told me that her cousin's holding her prisoner. Oh, illustrious ones, you must come back at once and find her.

THE FIRST GOD. This is terrible. Our whole search has come to grief. We didn't find many good people and those we found lived in a way quite unworthy of human beings. We'd already decided to confine ourselves to Shen Te.

THE SECOND GOD. If she's still good!

WANG. She certainly is, but she's disappeared!

THE FIRST GOD. Then all is lost.

THE SECOND GOD. Restrain yourself!

THE FIRST GOD. What good would that do? If she can't be found, we've got to retire. What sort of world did we find? Misery, vulgarity, and waste everywhere! Even the countryside has fallen away from us. The lovely trees are decapitated by telephone wires and on the other side of the mountains we see heavy smoke clouds and hear the thunder of cannon. And nowhere a good man who can pull through!

THE THIRD GOD. Alas, water seller, our commandments seem to be deadly. I fear that all our moral rules have to be done away with. People keep busy just saving their skins. Good intentions bring them to the brink of the abyss, and good deeds throw them into it. (*To the other two Gods*) The world can't be lived in, you've got to admit!

THE SECOND GOD (*vehemently*). No, it's people who are worthless!

THE THIRD GOD. The world is too cold!

THE SECOND GOD. People are too weak!

THE FIRST GOD. Dignity, my friends, dignity! Brothers, we mustn't despair. We did find one human being who was good and stayed good. She's only disappeared. Let's hurry and find her! One is enough! Didn't we say that everything can still turn out well if there's one human being who can stand this world? Just one?

(*They quickly disappear.*)

10

A courtroom. Groups: Mr. Shu Fu and the Landlady. Sun and his mother. Wang, the Carpenter, the Grandfather, the Young Prostitute, the Old Man and Woman. Mrs. Shin, the Policeman. The Unemployed, the Sister-in-law.

THE OLD MAN. He's too powerful.

WANG. He wants to open twelve new stores.

THE CARPENTER. How can the judge give a fair sentence if the accused's friends — the barber Shu Fu and the landlady Mi Tzu — are also *his* friends?

THE SISTER-IN-LAW. Mrs. Shin was seen last night carrying a fat goose into the judge's kitchen by order of Mr. Shui Ta. The fat was dripping through the basket.

THE OLD WOMAN (*to Wang*). Our poor Shen Te will never be found.

WANG. No, only the gods can discover the truth.

THE POLICEMAN. Order! The judges are coming!

(*Enter the three Gods in judges' robes. As they walk by the footlights on their way to their seats, one can hear them whispering.*)

THE THIRD GOD. We'll be found out. The certificates are very badly forged.

THE SECOND GOD. And people will wonder about the judge's sudden indigestion.

THE FIRST GOD. No, that's only natural. He ate half a goose.

MRS. SHIN. These are *new* judges!

WANG. And very good ones!

(*The third and last God hears this, turns round, and smiles at Wang. The Gods sit down. The First God beats on the table with a hammer. The Policeman brings in Shui Ta who is whistled at but walks with lordly steps.*)

THE POLICEMAN. Be prepared for a surprise. It isn't the just Fu Yi Tcheng. But the new judges look very mild too.

(*Shui Ta sees the Gods and faints.*)

THE YOUNG PROSTITUTE. What's the matter? The Tobacco King has fainted.

THE SISTER-IN-LAW. Yes, at the sight of the new judges!

WANG. He seems to know them! I don't understand that.

THE FIRST GOD. Are you the tobacco merchant Shui Ta?

SHUI TA (*weakly*). Yes.

THE FIRST GOD. You have been accused of doing away with your own cousin Miss Shen Te, in order to take possession of her business. Do you plead guilty?

SHUI TA. No.

THE FIRST GOD (*turning the pages of documents*). We'll first hear the policeman of this neighborhood on the reputation of the accused and on the reputation of his cousin.

THE POLICEMAN (*stepping forward*). Miss Shen Te was a girl who liked to please everyone, who lived and let live, as the saying goes. Mr. Shui Ta, on the other hand, is a man of principle. The generosity of Miss Shen Te forced him at times to strict measures. However, unlike the girl, he was always on the side of the law, your honor. Once, people to whom his cousin trustfully gave shelter were unmasked by him as a band of thieves. Another time he saved Miss Shen Te at the last moment from plain perjury. I know Mr. Shui Ta to be a respectable and law-abiding citizen.

THE FIRST GOD. Are there others present who want to testify that the accused is incapable of his supposed crime?

(*Mr. Shu Fu and the Landlady step forward.*)

THE POLICEMAN (*whispering to the Gods*). Mr. Shu Fu, a very influential gentleman.

MR. SHU FU. Mr. Shui Ta has the reputation of a highly respected businessman here in Setzuan. He is Vice-President of the Chamber of Commerce and is about to be made justice of the peace.

WANG (*interrupting*). By you! You're doing business with him!

THE POLICEMAN (*whispering*). A disagreeable character.

THE LANDLADY. As President of the Community Chest I'd like to call the attention of the court to this fact: Mr. Shui Ta is not only about to give to his numerous employees the best possible rooms, well-lighted and healthy, but is also making regular contributions to our home for the disabled.

THE POLICEMAN (*whispering*). Mrs. Mi Tzu, a close friend of the judge Fu Yi Tcheng!

THE FIRST GOD. Yes, yes, but now we've got to hear whether anyone has *less* favorable evidence to bring forward.

(*Wang, the Carpenter, the Old Man and Woman, the Unemployed, the Sister-in-law, and the Young Prostitute step forward.*)

THE POLICEMAN. The scum of the neighborhood.

THE FIRST GOD. Well, what do you know of the general behavior of Shui Ta?

SHOUTS (*jumbled*). He's ruined us!

— He blackmailed me!

— He led us off on the wrong track!

— Exploited the helpless!

— Lied!

— Cheated!

— Murdered!

THE FIRST GOD. Accused, what have you to say?

99

SHUI TA. I have simply enabled my cousin to exist, your honor. I only came when she was in danger of losing her little store. I had to come three times. I never wanted to stay. But the last time circumstances forced me to remain. I never had anything but trouble. My cousin was popular; I did the dirty work. That's why I'm hated.

THE SISTER-IN-LAW. You certainly are. Take our case, your honor! (*To Shui Ta*) I won't mention the sacks.

SHUI TA. Why not? Why not?

THE SISTER-IN-LAW (*to the Gods*). Shen Te gave us shelter and *he* had us arrested.

SHUI TA. You stole cakes!

THE SISTER-IN-LAW. Now he pretends to be interested in the baker's cakes! He wanted the store for himself!

SHUI TA. The store wasn't a public refuge, selfish creatures!

THE SISTER-IN-LAW. But we had no place to stay!

SHUI TA. There were too many of you!

WANG. And they (*pointing to the Old Man and Woman*) were selfish too?

THE OLD MAN. We put our savings into Shen Te's store. Why did you make us lose *our* store?

SHUI TA. Because my cousin was helping a flier to fly. I was to get the money!

WANG. Maybe she wanted to help him to fly. What interested you was the well-paid job in Peking. The store wasn't good enough for you!

SHUI TA. The rent was too high!

MRS. SHIN. That's true enough.

SHUI TA. And my cousin knew nothing about business!

MRS. SHIN. That's true too! She was also in love with the flier.

SHUI TA. Shouldn't she be allowed to love?

WANG. Certainly! And why did you want to force her to marry a man she did not love, the barber over there?

SHUI TA. The man she loved was a scoundrel.

WANG (*pointing to Sun*). Him?

SUN (*jumping up*). And because he was a scoundrel you took him into your office!

SHUI TA. To improve you! To improve you!

THE SISTER-IN-LAW. To make him into a slave-driver!

WANG. And when he was improved, didn't you sell him to her? (*Pointing to the Landlady*) She shouted it around every place!

SHUI TA. Because she wouldn't give me her buildings unless she had him to stroke her knees!

THE LANDLADY. That's a lie! Don't talk of my buildings ever again. I'll have nothing more to do with you. Murderer! (*She rustles off, insulted.*)

SUN (*insisting on getting his word in*). Your honor, I must speak on his behalf!

THE SISTER-IN-LAW. Naturally. You're in his employ.

THE UNEMPLOYED. He's the worst slave-driver I've ever known. He's absolutely depraved.

SUN. Your honor, the accused may have made whatever you say of me, but he's not a murderer. A few minutes before he was arrested I heard Shen Te's voice in his back room!

THE FIRST GOD (*avidly*). So she's alive? Tell us exactly what you heard?

SUN (*triumphantly*). Sobbing, your honor, sobbing!

THE THIRD GOD. And you recognized her?

SUN. Absolutely. How could I fail to recognize her voice?

MR. SHU FU. Sure, *you* made her sob often enough!

SUN. And yet I made her happy. But then he (*pointing to Shui Ta*) wanted to sell her to you!

SHUI TA (*to Sun*). Because you didn't love her!

WANG. No. For the money!

SHUI TA. But what was the money needed for, your honor? (*To Sun*) You wanted her to sacrifice all her friends, but the barber offered his cabins and his money to help the poor. Moreover, I *had* to get her engaged to him so that she could still be good.

WANG. Why didn't you let her be good when the big check was signed? Why did you send Shen Te's friends into the dirty sweatshops of your factory, Tobacco King?

SHUI TA. For the child's sake!

101

THE CARPENTER. And *my* children? What did you do with *my* children?

(*Shui Ta is silent.*)

WANG. Now you're silent! The gods gave the store to Shen Te as a little fountain of goodness. She always wanted to do good and you always came and spoiled it.

SHUI TA (*beside himself*). Because otherwise the fountain would have dried up, fool!

MRS. SHIN. That's true, your honor!

WANG. What good is a fountain if you can't get at the water?

SHUI TA. Good deeds mean ruin!

WANG (*wildly*). But bad deeds mean a good life, don't they? What did you do with the good Shen Te, bad man? How many good people are there, illustrious ones? *She* was good! When that man over there smashed my hand, she wanted to testify for me. And now I testify for her. She was good, I swear! (*He raises his hand in an oath.*)

THE THIRD GOD. What's the matter with your hand, water seller? It's all stiff.

WANG (*pointing to Shui Ta*). It's his fault, his alone! She wanted to give me money for the doctor but then *he* came along! You were her deadly enemy!

SHUI TA. I was her only friend!

ALL. Where is she?

SHUI TA. Gone away!

WANG. Where to?

SHUI TA. I won't tell!

ALL. And why did she have to go away?

SHUI TA (*shouting*). Because you would have torn her to shreds! (*Sudden quiet. He sinks onto a chair*) I can't go on. I'll explain everything. If the hall is cleared and only the judges remain, I will make a confession.

ALL. He's confessing! He's found out!

THE FIRST GOD (*beating on the table with the hammer*). Let the hall be cleared!

(*The Policeman clears the hall.*)

MRS. SHIN (*laughing as she goes*). There'll be a surprise!

102

SHUI TA. Have they gone? All of them? I can no longer keep
silence. I recognized you, illustrious ones!
THE SECOND GOD. What did you do with our good woman of
Setzuan?
SHUI TA. Let me confess the terrible truth: I am she!
THE SECOND GOD. Shen Te!
SHEN TE.

Yes, it is I. Shui Ta and Shen Te. I am both.
Your former injunction to be good and yet to live
Tore me like lightning in halves.
I don't know how it happened.
To be good to others and to myself —
I couldn't do both at the same time.
To help others and to help myself was too hard.
Alas, your world is difficult! Too much misery, too
much despair!
The hand that is extended to a beggar, the beggar at
once tears off!
Whoever helps the lost is lost himself!
For who could long refuse to be bad when he who
eats no meat must die?
All the things that were needed — where should I
have taken them from?
From myself! But then I perished!
A load of good intentions weighed me down to the
ground.
Yet when I was unjust I walked mightily about and
ate good meat!
Something must be wrong with your world.
Why is malice well rewarded? Why do punishments
await the good?
Oh, how I should have loved to pamper myself!
And there was also a secret knowledge in me.
My foster-mother washed me in water from the gutter:
That gave me a sharp eye.
Yet pity pained me so, I was an angry wolf at the
sight of misery.

103

Then I felt how I was changing and kind words
    turned to ashes in my mouth.
And yet I wished to be an Angel to the Suburbs.
To give was a delight. A happy face, and I walked
    on clouds.
Condemn me: everything I did I did to help my
    neighbor,
To love my lover, and to save my little son from
    want.
For your great plans, O gods! I was too poor and
    small.

THE FIRST GOD (*with all signs of horror*). Don't go on, unhappy woman! What should we think, we who are so happy to have found you again!

SHEN TE. But I've got to tell you that I am the bad man whose crimes everyone was talking about!

THE FIRST GOD. The good woman whose good deeds everyone was talking about!

SHEN TE. The bad man too!

THE FIRST GOD. A misunderstanding! Several unfortunate occurrences! Some heartless neighbors! An excess of zeal!

THE SECOND GOD. But how is she to go on living?

THE FIRST GOD. She can do it. She's strong, well built. She can stand a lot.

THE SECOND GOD. But didn't you hear what she said?

THE FIRST GOD (*vehemently*). It was confused, very confused! And incredible, highly incredible! Should we admit our commandments to be deadly? Should we renounce our commandments? (*Sullenly*) Never! Should the world be changed? How? By whom? No! Everything is in order! (*He suddenly beats on the table with the hammer.*)

And now . . . (*He makes a sign and music is heard. Rosy light.*) let us return.
This little world has much engaged us.
Its joy and its sorrow have refreshed and pained us.
Up there, however, beyond the stars,
We shall gladly think of you, Shen Te, the good woman

Who bears witness to our spirit down below,
Who, in cold darkness, carries a little lamp!
Goodbye! Do it well!

(*He makes a sign and the ceiling opens. A pink cloud comes down. On it the Three Gods rise, very slowly.*)

SHEN TE. Oh, don't, illustrious ones! Don't go away! Don't leave me! How can I face the good old couple who've lost their store and the water seller with his stiff hand? And how can I defend myself from the barber whom I do not love and from Sun whom I do love? And I am with child. Soon there'll be a little son who'll want to eat. I can't stay here! (*She turns with a hunted look toward the door which will let her tormentors in.*)

THE FIRST GOD. You can do it. Just be good and everything will turn out well!

(*Enter the witnesses. They look with surprise at the judges floating on their pink cloud.*)

WANG. Show respect! The gods have appeared among us! Three of the highest gods have come to Setzuan to find a good human being. They had found one already, but . . .

THE FIRST GOD. No "but"! Here she is!

ALL. Shen Te!

THE FIRST GOD. She has not perished. She was only hidden. She will stay with you. A good human being!

SHEN TE. But I need my cousin!

THE FIRST GOD. Not too often!

SHEN TE. At least once a week!

THE FIRST GOD. Once a month. That's enough!

SHEN TE. Oh, don't go away, illustrious ones! I haven't told you everything! I need you desperately!

(*The Gods sing.*)

THE TRIO OF THE VANISHING GODS ON THE CLOUD

Unhappily we cannot stay
More than a fleeting year.
If we watch our find too long
It will disappear.

Here the golden light of truth
With shadow is alloyed
Therefore now we ask your leave
To go back to our void.

SHEN TE. Help! (*Her cries continue through the song.*)
Since our search is over now
Let us fast ascend!
The good woman of Setzuan
Praise we at the end!

(*As Shen Te stretches out her arms to them in desperation,
they disappear above, smiling and waving.*)

EPILOGUE

One of the actors walks out in front of the curtain and apologetically addresses the audience.

Ladies and gentlemen, don't be angry! Please!
We know the play is still in need of mending.
A golden legend floated on the breeze,
The breeze dropped, and we got a bitter ending.
Being dependent on your approbation
We wished, alas! our work might be commended.
We're disappointed too. With consternation
We see the curtain closed, the plot unended.
In your opinion, then, what's to be done?
Change human nature or — the world? Well: which?
Believe in bigger, better gods or — none?
How can we mortals be both good and rich?
The right way out of the calamity
You must find for yourselves. Ponder, my friends,
How man with man may live in amity
And good men — women also — reach good ends.
There must, there must, be *some* end that would fit.
Ladies and gentlemen, help us look for it!

106

THE CAUCASIAN CHALK CIRCLE

THE JUDGE. Officer, fetch a piece of chalk. You will trace below the bench a circle, in the center of which you will place the young child. Then you will order the two women to wait, each of them at opposite sides of the circle. When the real mother takes hold of him, it will be easy for the child to come outside the circle. But the pretended mother cannot lead him out.

(*The officer traces a circle with the chalk and motions the child to stand in the center of it. Mrs. Ma takes the child's hand and leads him out of the circle. Hai-Tang fails to contend with her.*)

THE JUDGE. It is evident that Hai-Tang is not the mother of the child, since she did not come forward to draw him out of the circle.

HAI-TANG. I supplicate you, Honored Sir, to calm your wrath. If I cannot obtain my son without dislocating his arm or bruising his baby flesh, I would rather perish under the blows than make the least effort to take him out of the circle.

THE JUDGE. A sage of old once said: What man can hide what he really is? Behold the power of the Chalk Circle! In order to seize an inheritance, Mrs. Ma has raised a young child that is not her own. But the Chalk Circle augustly brought out the truth and the falsehood. Mrs. Ma has an engaging exterior but her heart is corrupt. The true mother — Hai-Tang — is at last recognized.

From *The Chalk Circle*, an anonymous Chinese play of about 1300 A.D.

PART ONE

1

THE NOBLE CHILD

As the lights go up, a Story Teller is seen sitting on the floor, a black sheepskin cloak round his shoulders, and a little, well-thumbed notebook in his hand. A small group of listeners — the chorus — sits with him. The manner of his recitation makes it clear that he has told this story over and over again. He mechanically fingers the pages, seldom looking at them. With appropriate gestures, he gives the signal for each scene to begin.

THE STORY TELLER.

> In olden times, in a bloody time,
> There ruled in a Caucasian city —
> Men called it the City of the Damned —
> A governor.
> His name was Georgi Abashwili.
> He was rich as Croesus
> He had a beautiful wife
> He had a healthy child.
> No other governor in Grusinia
> Had so many horses in his stable
> So many beggars on his doorstep
> So many soldiers in his service
> So many petitioners in his courtyard.
> Georgi Abashwili — how shall I describe him?

He enjoyed his life.
On the morning of Easter Sunday
The Governor and his family went to church.

(*At the left a large doorway, at the right an even larger gateway. Beggars and petitioners pour from the gateway, holding up thin children, crutches, and petitions. They are followed by two Ironshirts, and then, expensively dressed, the Governor's family.*)

BEGGARS AND PETITIONERS. Mercy! Mercy, Your Grace! The taxes are way up, we can't pay!

— I lost my leg in the Persian War, where can I get . . .

— My brother is innocent, Your Grace, there's been a misunderstanding . . .

— The child is starving in my arms!

— We plead for our son's discharge from the army, our last remaining son!

— Please, Your Grace, the water inspector takes bribes.

(*One servant collects the petitions, another distributes coins from a purse. Soldiers push the crowd back, lashing at them with thick leather whips.*)

THE SOLDIER. Get back! Clear the church door!

(*Behind the Governor, his Wife, and the Adjutant, the Governor's child is brought through the gateway in an ornate carriage.*)

THE CROWD. The child!

— I can't see it, don't shove so hard!

— God bless the child, Your Grace!

THE STORY TELLER (*while the crowd is driven back with whips*).

> For the first time on that Easter Sunday, the people
> saw the Governor's heir.
> Two doctors never moved from the noble child, apple
> of the Governor's eye.
> Even the mighty Prince Kazbeki bows before it at the
> Church door.

(*A fat prince steps forward and greets the family.*)

THE FAT PRINCE. Happy Easter, Natella Abashwili! A magnificent day! When it was raining in the night, I thought to myself: gloomy holidays! But this morning I said to myself: the sky is gay! I love a gay sky, a simple heart, Natella Abashwili. And little Michael is a governor from head to foot! Tititi! (*He tickles the child.*)

THE GOVERNOR'S WIFE. What do you thing of this, Arsen? At last Georgi has decided to start building the wing on the east side. All those wretched slums and suburbs are to be torn down to make room for a garden.

THE FAT PRINCE. That's good news after so much bad! What's the latest about the war, Brother Georgi? (*The Governor indicates a lack of interest.*) A strategical retreat, I hear. Well, minor reverses are to be expected. Sometimes things go well, sometimes not. Such is war! What difference does it make?

THE GOVERNOR'S WIFE. He's coughing. Georgi, did you hear? (*She speaks sharply to the Doctors, two dignified men standing close to the little carriage.*) He's coughing!

THE FIRST DOCTOR (*to the second*). May I remind you, Niko Mikadze, that I was against the lukewarm bath? (*To the Governor's Wife*) There's been a little error over warming the bath water, Your Grace.

THE SECOND DOCTOR (*equally polite*). Mika Loladze, I can't possibly agree with you. The temperature of the bath water was the one prescribed by our great, beloved Mishiko Oboladze. It was more likely a slight draft during the night, Your Grace.

THE GOVERNOR'S WIFE. But do pay more attention to him. He looks feverish, Georgi.

THE FIRST DOCTOR (*bending over the child*). No cause for alarm, Your Grace. The bath water will be warmer. It won't occur again.

THE SECOND DOCTOR (*with a venomous glance at the first*). I won't forget that, my dear Mika Loladze. No cause for concern, Your Grace.

THE FAT PRINCE. Well, well, well! I always say: One pain in my liver and the doctor gets fifty strokes on the soles of his feet. That's because we are living in a decadent age. In the old days one simply said: Off with his head!

111

THE GOVERNOR'S WIFE. Let's go into the church. Very likely it's the draft here.

(*The procession of family and servants turns into the doorway. The Fat Prince follows, but the Governor is kept back by the Adjutant, a handsome young man. When the crowd of petitioners has been driven off, a young dust-stained rider, his arm in a sling, remains behind.*)

THE ADJUTANT (*pointing at the rider, who steps forward*). Won't you listen to the messenger from the Capital. Your Excellency? He arrived this morning. With confidential papers.

THE GOVERNOR. Not before Service, Shalva. But did you hear Brother Kazbeki bid me a happy Easter? That's all very well, but so far as I know, it didn't rain here last night.

THE ADJUTANT (*nodding*). That will have to be gone into.

THE GOVERNOR. Yes, at once. Tomorrow.

(*They pass through the doorway. The rider, who has waited in vain for an audience, turns sharply round and, muttering a curse, goes off. Only one of the Palace Guards — Simon Shashava — remains at the door.*)

THE STORY TELLER.

> On the church square the pigeons are strutting.
> The city lies still.
> A soldier of the Palace Guard
> Is joking with a kitchen maid
> As she comes up from the river with a bundle.

(*A girl — Grusha Vashnadze — comes through the gateway with a bundle made of large green leaves under her arm.*)

SIMON. What, the young lady is not in church? Shirking?

GRUSHA. I was dressed to go. But they needed another goose for the banquet. And they asked me to go and get it. I know something about geese.

SIMON. A goose? (*He feigns suspicion.*) I'd like to see that goose. (*Grusha does not understand.*) One has to be on one's guard with women. "I only went for a fish," they tell you, and then it turns out to be something else.

GRUSHA (*walking resolutely toward him and showing him the goose*). There it is. And if it isn't a fifteen-pound goose stuffed full of corn, I'll eat the feathers.

112

SIMON. A queen of a goose. The Governor himself will eat it. So the young lady has been down to the river again?

GRUSHA. Yes, at the poultry farm.

SIMON. Really? At the poultry farm, down by the river . . . not higher up maybe? Near those willows?

GRUSHA. I only go to the willows to wash the linen.

SIMON (*insinuatingly*). Exactly.

GRUSHA. Exactly what?

SIMON (*winking*). Exactly that.

GRUSHA. Why shouldn't I wash the linen by the willows?

SIMON (*with exaggerated laughter*). Why shouldn't I wash the linen by the willows! That's good, really good!

GRUSHA. I don't understand the soldier. What's so good about it?

SIMON (*slyly*). "If something *I* know someone learns, she'll grow hot and cold by turns!"

GRUSHA. I don't know what I *could* learn about those willows.

SIMON. Not even if there were a bush opposite? And everything could be seen from it? Everything that goes on there when a certain person is — er — "washing linen"?

GRUSHA. What *is* it that goes on? Won't the soldier say what he means and have done with it?

SIMON. Something goes on. And something can be seen.

GRUSHA. Could the soldier mean I put my toes in the water? When it was hot once in a while? There wasn't anything else.

SIMON. There were the toes. And more.

GRUSHA. More what? At most the foot?

SIMON. The foot. And a little more. (*He laughs heartily.*)

GRUSHA (*angrily*). Simon Shashava, you ought to be ashamed of yourself! To sit in a bush and wait till someone comes along and puts her leg in the river on a hot day! And with another soldier very likely! (*She runs off.*)

SIMON (*shouting after her*). Not with another soldier!

(*As the Story Teller resumes his tale, the soldier steps into the doorway as though to listen to the service.*)

THE STORY TELLER.

The city lies still, but why are there armed men?
The Governor's Palace is at peace,
But why is it a fortress?

113

And the Governor returned to his Palace
And the fortress was a trap
And the goose was plucked and roasted
And the goose was not eaten any more
And noon was no longer the time to eat
Noon was the time to die.

(*From the doorway at the left the Fat Prince quickly appears, stands still, looks around. Before the gateway at the right two Ironshirts are squatting and playing dice. The Fat Prince sees them, walks slowly past, making a sign to them. They rise: one goes through the gateway, the other goes off at the right. Muffled voices are heard from various directions in the rear: "To your posts!" The Palace is surrounded. The Fat Prince quickly goes off. Church bells in the distance. Enter, through the doorway, the Governor's family and procession, returning from Church.*)

THE GOVERNOR'S WIFE (*passing the Adjutant*). It's really impossible to live in this slum. But Georgi, of course, always builds only for his little Michael. Never for me. Michael is all! All for Michael!

(*The procession turns into the gateway. Again the Adjutant lingers behind. He waits. Enter the wounded rider from the doorway. Two Ironshirts of the Palace Guard have taken up positions by the gateway.*)

THE ADJUTANT (*to the rider*). The Governor doesn't wish to receive military reports before dinner — particularly if they are of a depressing nature, as I assume. In the afternoon His Excellency will devote himself to conferences with prominent architects who are also invited to dinner. Here they are already. (*Enter three gentlemen through the doorway.*) Go to the kitchen and get yourself something to eat, friend. (*As the rider goes, the Adjutant greets the Architects.*) Gentlemen, His Excellency expects you at dinner. All his time will be devoted to you. To your great new plans! Come, quickly!

ONE OF THE ARCHITECTS. We marvel that His Excellency intends to build. There are disquieting rumors abroad that the war in Persia has taken a bad turn.

114

THE ADJUTANT. All the more reason to build! That's nothing, you know. Persia is a long way off. The garrison here would let itself be hacked to bits for its Governor. (*Noise from the palace. The shrill scream of a woman. Someone is shouting orders. Dumbfounded, the Adjutant moves toward the gateway. An Ironshirt steps out, points his lance at him.*) What's going on here? Put down that lance, you dog!

ONE OF THE ARCHITECTS. The Princes! Don't you realize that the Princes met last night in the capital? And that they are against the Grand Duke and his Governors? Gentlemen, we'd better make ourselves scarce. (*They rush off. The Adjutant remains helplessly behind.*)

THE ADJUTANT (*furiously to the Palace Guard*). Lay down your arms. Don't you realize an attempt is being made on the Governor's life?

(*The Ironshirts of the Palace Guard refuse to obey. They stare coldly and indifferently at the Adjutant and follow the next events without interest.*)

THE STORY TELLER.

O blindness of great ones!
They wander like gods,
Great over bent backs,
Sure of hired fists,
Trusting in the power
Which has lasted so long.
But long is not forever.
O change from age to age!
Thou hope of the people!

(*Enter the Governor, through the gateway, between two soldiers fully armed. He is in chains. His face is gray.*)

Up, great sir, deign to walk upright!
From your palace the eyes of many foes follow you!
You no longer need an architect, a carpenter will do!
You will not move into a new palace,
But into a little hole in the ground.
Look about you once more, blind man!

115

(*The arrested man looks round.*)

Does all you had please you?
Between the Easter mass and the Easter meal
You are walking to the place whence no one returns.

(*The Governor is led off. A horn sounds an alarm. Noise behind the gateway.*)

When the house of a great one collapses
Many little ones are slain.
Those who had no share in the *good* fortunes of
    the mighty
Often have a share in their *mis*fortunes.
The plunging wagon
Drags the sweating beasts with it
Into the abyss.

(*The servants come rushing through the gateway in panic.*)

THE SERVANTS (*among themselves*). The baskets!
— Take them all into the third courtyard! Food for five days!
— The mistress has fainted! Someone must carry her down. She must get away.
— What about us? We'll be slaughtered like chickens, that's how it always is.
— Goodness gracious, what'll happen? There's bloodshed already in the city, they say.
— Nonsense, the Governor has just been politely asked to appear at a Princes' meeting. Everything'll be ironed out. I heard this on the best authority . . .

(*The two doctors rush into the courtyard.*)

THE FIRST DOCTOR (*trying to restrain the other*). Niko Mikadze, it is your duty as a doctor to attend Natella Abashwili.

THE SECOND DOCTOR. My duty! It's yours!

THE FIRST DOCTOR. Whose turn is it to look after the child today, Niko Mikadze, yours or mine?

THE SECOND DOCTOR. Do you really think, Mika Loladze, I'm going to stay one minute longer in this blasted house on that little brat's account?

116

(*They start fighting. All one hears is:* "You neglect your duty!" *and* "Duty here, duty there!" *Then the Second Doctor knocks the first down.*)

THE SECOND DOCTOR. Oh, go to hell! (*Exit.*)

(*Enter the soldier, Simon Shashava. He searches in the crowd for Grusha.*)

THE SERVANTS. There's still time before tonight. The soldiers won't be drunk till then.

—Does anyone know if the mutiny has begun?

—The Palace Guard has ridden off.

—Doesn't anybody know what's happened?

GRUSHA. Meliva the fisherman says a comet with a red tail has been seen in the sky over the capital. That means bad luck.

THE SERVANTS. Yesterday they were saying in the capital that the Persian War is lost.

— The Princes have staged a big uprising.

— There's a rumor that the Grand Duke has already fled.

— All his governors are to be executed.

— The little people will be left alone.

— I have a brother with the Ironshirts.

THE ADJUTANT (*appearing in the doorway*). Everyone get into the third courtyard! Everyone help with the packing!

(*He drives the servants away. At last Simon finds Grusha.*)

SIMON. Grusha! There you are at last! What are you going to do?

GRUSHA. Nothing. If the worst comes to the worst, I've a brother in the mountains. What about you?

SIMON. There is nothing to say about me. (*Formally again*) Grusha Vashnadze, your desire to know my plans fills me with satisfaction. I have been ordered to accompany Madam Natella Abashwili as her guard.

GRUSHA. But hasn't the Palace Guard mutinied?

SIMON (*seriously*). That's a fact.

GRUSHA. But isn't it dangerous to accompany the woman?

SIMON. In Tiflis, they say: Is not the stabbing dangerous for the knife?

GRUSHA. You're not a knife. You're a man, Simon Shashava. What has the woman got to do with you?

117

SIMON. The woman has nothing to do with me. I have my orders, and I go.

GRUSHA. The soldier is pigheaded: he gets himself into danger for nothing — nothing at all. Now I must go into the third courtyard. I'm in a hurry.

SIMON. Since we're in a hurry we shouldn't quarrel. You need time for a good quarrel. May I ask if the young lady still has parents?

GRUSHA. No, only a brother.

SIMON. As time is short — the second question is this: Is the young lady as healthy as a fish in water?

GRUSHA. Maybe once in a while I have a pain in the right shoulder. Otherwise I'm strong enough for my job. No one has complained. So far.

SIMON. Everyone knows that. Even if it's Easter Sunday, and there's a question who should run for the goose, she's the one. The third question is this: Is the young lady impatient? Does she want apples in winter?

GRUSHA. Impatient? No. But if a man goes to war without any reason and no message arrives — that's bad.

SIMON. A message will come. And now the final question . . .

GRUSHA. Simon Shashava, I've got to go to the third courtyard and hurry. My answer is yes.

SIMON (*very embarrassed*). Haste, they say, is the name of the wind that blows down the scaffolding. But they also say: The rich don't know what haste is. I'm from . . .

GRUSHA. Kutsk . . .

SIMON. So the young lady has already inquired about me? I'm healthy, have no dependents, make ten piasters a month, as a paymaster twenty piasters, and am asking — very sincerely — for your hand.

GRUSHA. Simon Shashava, it suits me.

SIMON (*taking from his neck a thin chain with a little cross on it*). My mother gave me this cross, Grusha Vashnadze. The chain is silver. Please wear it.

GRUSHA. Many thanks, Simon. (*He hangs it round her neck.*)

SIMON. It would be better for the young lady to go into the third

118

courtyard now. Or there will be difficulties. Anyway, I have to harness the horses. The young lady will understand.

GRUSHA. Yes, Simon.

(*They stand undecided.*)

SIMON. I'll only take the mistress to the troops that have remained loyal. When the war's over, I'll be back. In two weeks. Or three. I hope my intended won't get tired, waiting my return.

GRUSHA. Simon Shashava, I shall wait for you.

> Go calmly into battle, soldier
> The bloody battle, the bitter battle
> From which not everyone returns:
> When you return I shall be there.
> I shall be waiting for you under the green elm
> I shall be waiting for you under the bare elm
> I shall wait until the last soldier has returned
> And longer.
> When you come back from the battle
> No boots will lie before the door
> The pillow beside mine will be empty
> And my mouth will be unkissed.
> When you return, when you return
> You will be able to say: All is as it was.

SIMON. I thank you, Grusha Vashnadze. And goodbye!

(*He bows low before her. She does the same before him. Then she runs quickly off without looking round. Enter the Adjutant from the gateway.*)

THE ADJUTANT (*harshly*). Harness the horses to the carriage! Don't stand there doing nothing, louse!

(*Simon Shashava stands to attention and goes off. Two servants crawl from the gateway, bent low under huge trunks. Behind them, supported by her women, stumbles Natella Abashwili. She is followed by a woman carrying the child.*)

THE GOVERNOR'S WIFE. I hardly know if my head's still on. Where's Michael? Don't hold him so clumsily. Pile the trunks onto the carriage. Shalva, is there any news from the city?

119

THE ADJUTANT. No. So far, all is quiet. But there's not a minute to lose. There's not enough room for the trunks in the carriage. Pick out what you need. (*Exit quickly.*)

THE GOVERNOR'S WIFE. Only essentials! Quick, open the trunks. I'll tell you what I've got to have. (*The trunks are lowered and opened. She points at some brocade dresses.*) The green one! And of course the one with the fur trimming. Where are Niko Mikadze and Mika Loladze? I've suddenly got the most terrible migraine again. It always starts in the temples. (*Enter Grusha.*) You're taking your time, eh? Go at once and get the hot water bottles. (*Grusha runs off, returns later with hot water bottles. The Governor's Wife orders her about by signs.*) Don't tear the sleeves.

A YOUNG WOMAN. Pardon, madam, no harm has come to the dress.

THE GOVERNOR'S WIFE. Because I stopped you. I've been watching you for a long time. Nothing in your head but making eyes at Shalva Tzereteli. I'll kill you, you bitch! (*She beats the woman.*)

THE ADJUTANT (*appearing in the gateway*). I must ask you to make haste, Natella Abashwili. Firing has broken out in the city. (*Exit.*)

THE GOVERNOR'S WIFE (*letting go of the young woman*). Oh dear, do you think they'll do something to us? Why should they? Why? (*She herself begins to rummage in the trunks.*) How's Michael? Asleep?

THE WOMAN WITH THE CHILD. Yes, madam.

THE GOVERNOR'S WIFE. Then put him down a moment and get my little saffron-colored boots from the bedchamber. I need them for the green dress. (*The woman puts down the child and goes off.*) Just look how these things have been packed! No love! No understanding! If you don't give them every order yourself . . . At such moments you realize what kind of servants you have! They gorge themselves, and never a word of gratitude! I'll remember this.

THE ADJUTANT (*entering, very excited*). Natella, you must leave at once!

120

THE GOVERNOR'S WIFE. Why? I've got to take this silver dress
— it cost a thousand piasters. And that one there, and where's
the wine-colored one?

THE ADJUTANT (*trying to pull her away*). Riots have broken
out! We've got to leave right now. Where's the child?

THE GOVERNOR'S WIFE (*calling to the young woman who was
holding the child*). Maro, get the child ready! Where on
earth are you?

THE ADJUTANT (*leaving*). We'll probably have to do without
the carriage and go on horseback.

(*The Governor's Wife rummages again among her dresses,
throws some onto the heap of chosen clothes, then takes them
off again. Noises, drums are heard. The young woman who
was beaten creeps away. The sky begins to grow red.*)

THE GOVERNOR'S WIFE (*rummaging desperately*). I simply cannot find the wine-colored dress. Take the whole pile and
carry it as it is to the carriage. Where's Asja? And why
hasn't Maro come back? Have you all gone crazy?

THE ADJUTANT (*returning*). Quick! Quick!

THE GOVERNOR'S WIFE (*to the first woman*). Run! Just throw
them into the carriage!

THE ADJUTANT. We are not going by carriage. Come at once
or I'll ride off on my own!

THE GOVERNOR'S WIFE (*as the first woman can't carry everything*). Where's that bitch, Asja? (*The Adjutant pulls her
away.*) Maro, bring the child! (*To the first woman*) Go and
look for Masha. No, first take the dresses to the carriage.
Such nonsense, I wouldn't dream of going on horseback!
(*Turning round, she sees the red sky, and starts back rigid.
The fire burns. She is pulled out by the Adjutant. Shaking,
the first woman follows with the dresses.*)

MARO (*from the doorway with the boots*). Madam! (*She sees
the trunks and dresses and runs toward the child, picks it
up, and holds it a moment.*) They left it behind, the beasts.
(*She hands it to Grusha.*) Hold it a moment. (*She runs off,
following the Governor's Wife. Enter servants from the gateway.*)

121

THE COOK. Well, they've actually gone. Without the food wagons, and not a minute too early. Now it's time to get out!

A GROOM. This is going to be an unhealthy house for some time. (*To one of the women*) Suliko, take a few blankets and wait for me in the foal stables.

GRUSHA. What have they done to the Governor?

THE GROOM (*gesturing throat cutting*). Fffffft.

A FAT WOMAN (*seeing the gesture and becoming hysterical*). Oh dear, oh dear, oh dear, oh dear! Our master Georgi Abashwili! A picture of health he was, at the Morning Mass — and now! Oh, take me away, we're all lost! We must die in sin! Like our master, Georgi Abashwili!

THE OTHER WOMEN (*soothing her*). Calm down, Nina! You'll be taken to safety. You've never done anyone any harm.

THE FAT WOMAN (*being led out*). Oh dear, oh dear, oh dear! Quick! Let's all get out before they come. Before they come!

A YOUNG WOMAN. Nina takes it more to heart than the mistress, that's a fact. *They* even have to have their *weeping* done for them.

THE COOK. We'd better get out, all of us.

ANOTHER WOMAN (*glancing back*). That must be the East Gate burning.

THE YOUNG WOMAN (*seeing the child in Grusha's arms*). The child! What are *you* doing with it?

GRUSHA. It's been left behind.

THE YOUNG WOMAN. She simply left it! Michael, who was kept out of all the drafts!

(*The servants gather round the child.*)

GRUSHA. He's waking up.

THE GROOM. Better put him down, I tell you. I'd rather not think what'd happen to anybody who's seen with that child.

THE COOK. That's right. Once they start, they'll kill each other off, whole families at a time. Let's go.

(*Exeunt all but Grusha, with the child on her arm, and two women.*)

THE TWO WOMEN. Didn't you hear? Better put him down.

GRUSHA. The nurse asked me to hold him a moment.

THE OLDER WOMAN. She'll never come back, you simpleton.

THE YOUNGER WOMAN. Keep your hands off it.

THE OLDER WOMAN (*amiably*). Grusha, you're a good soul, but you're not very bright and you know it. I tell you, if he had the plague it couldn't be worse.

GRUSHA (*stubbornly*). He hasn't got the plague. He looks at me! He's human!

THE OLDER WOMAN. Don't look at *him*. You are a fool — just the kind that always gets put upon. Someone says to you "Run for the salad, you have the longest legs," and you run. My husband has an ox cart — you can come with us if you hurry! Lord, by now the whole neighborhood must be in flames.

(*Both women leave, sighing. After some hesitation, Grusha puts the sleeping child down, looks at it for a moment, then takes a brocade blanket from the heap of clothes and covers it. Then both women return, dragging bundles. Grusha starts guiltily away from the child and walks a few steps to one side.*)

THE YOUNGER WOMAN. Haven't you packed anything yet? There isn't much time, you know. The Ironshirts will be here from the barracks.

GRUSHA. Coming.

(*She runs through the doorway. Both women go to the gateway and wait. The sound of horses is heard. They flee, screaming. Enter the Fat Prince with drunken Ironshirts. One of them carries the Governor's head on a lance.*)

THE FAT PRINCE. Here! In the middle! (*One soldier climbs onto the other's back, takes the head, holds it tentatively over the door.*) That's not the middle. Farther to the right. That's it. What I do, my friends, I do well. (*While, with hammer and nail, the soldier fastens the head to the wall by its hair*) This morning at the Church door I said to Georgi Abashwili: "I love a clear sky." Actually I prefer the lightning that comes out of a clear sky. Yes indeed. It's a pity they took the brat along, though. I need him. Urgently.

(*Exit with Ironshirts through the gateway. Trampling of*

horses again. Enter Grusha through the doorway looking cau-
tiously about her. Clearly she has waited for the Ironshirts
to go. Carrying a bundle, she walks toward the gateway. At
the last moment, she turns to see if the child is still there.
Catching sight of the head over the doorway, she screams.
Horrified, she picks up her bundle again, and is about to
leave when the Story Teller starts to speak. She stands rooted
to the spot.)

THE STORY TELLER.

As she was standing between courtyard and gate,
She heard or she thought she heard a low voice calling;
The child called to her,
Not whining, but calling quite sensibly,
At least so it seemed to her.
"Woman," it said, "help me."
And it went on, not whining, but saying quite sensibly:
"Know, woman, he who hears not a cry for help
But passes by with troubled ears will never hear
The gentle call of a lover nor the blackbird at dawn
Nor the happy sigh of the exhausted grape-picker
As the Angelus rings."

(She walks a few steps toward the child and bends over it.)

Hearing this she went back for one more look
    at the child.
Only to sit with him for a moment or two,
Only till someone should come,
Its mother, perhaps, or anyone else.

(Leaning on a trunk, she sits facing the child.)

Only till she would have to leave, for the danger
    was too great,
The city was full of flame and crying.

*(The light grows dimmer, as though evening and night were
coming on.)*

Terrible is the temptation of goodness!

*(Grusha now settles down to watch over the child through the
night. Once, she lights a small lamp to look at it. Once, she*

tucks it in with a coat. From time to time she listens and looks to see whether someone is coming.)

A long time she sat with the child
Till evening came, till night came, till dawn
  came.
Too long she sat, too long she saw
The soft breathing, the little fists,
Till toward morning the temptation grew too
  strong
And she rose, and bent down and, sighing,
  took the child
And carried it off.

(*She does what the Story Teller says as he describes it.*)

Like plunder she took it to herself
Like a thief she crept away.

2

THE FLIGHT INTO THE NORTHERN MOUNTAINS

THE STORY TELLER.

As Grusha Vashnadze left the city
On the Grusinian highway
On the way to the Northern Mountains
She sang a song, she bought some milk.

THE CHORUS.

How will this human child escape
The bloodhounds, the trap-setters?
Into the deserted mountains she journeyed
Along the Grusinian highway she journeyed
She sang a song, she bought some milk.

(*Grusha Vashnadze walks on. On her back she carries the child in a sack, in one hand is a large stick, in the other a bundle. She sings.*)

THE SONG OF THE FOUR GENERALS
Four generals
Set out for Baku.
The first no war had ever begun
The second fought but never won
For the third no weather was ever right
For the fourth the men would never fight
Four generals
And none got through.

Sosso Robakidse
Marched to Iran
A mighty war he'd soon begun
A mighty battle he'd soon won
For him the weather was always right
For him the men would always fight
Sosso Robakidse
Is our man!

(*A peasant's cottage appears.*)

GRUSHA (*to the child*). Noontime is eating time. Now we'll sit hopefully in the grass, while the good Grusha goes and buys a little pitcher of milk. (*She lays the child down and knocks at the cottage door. An old man opens it.*) Grandfather, could I have a little pitcher of milk? And a corn cake, maybe?

THE OLD MAN. Milk? We haven't any milk. The soldiers from the city have our goats. Go to the soldiers if you want milk.

GRUSHA. But grandfather, you must have a little pitcher of milk for a child?

THE OLD MAN. And for a God-bless-you, eh?

GRUSHA. Who said anything about a God-bless-you? (*She shows her purse.*) We're going to pay like princes. "The head in the clouds, the behind in the water." (*The peasant goes off grumbling for milk.*) How much for this little pitcher?

126

THE OLD MAN. Three piasters. Milk has gone up.

GRUSHA. Three piasters for that little drop? (*Without a word the Old Man shuts the door in her face.*) Michael, did you hear that? Three piasters! We can't afford it! (*She goes back, sits down again, and gives the child her breast.*) Suck. Think of the three piasters. There's nothing there, but you *think* you're drinking, and that's something. (*Shaking her head, she sees that the child isn't sucking any more. She gets up, walks back to the door, and knocks again.*) Open, grandfather, we'll pay. (*Softly*) May lightning strike you! (*When the Old Man appears*) I thought it would be half a piaster. But the child must have something. What about one piaster for that little drop?

THE OLD MAN. Two.

GRUSHA. Don't shut the door again. (*She fishes a long time in her bag.*) Here are two piasters. But milk has got to go down again. I still have two days' journey ahead of me. This is a murderous business and a sin too!

THE OLD MAN. Kill the soldiers if you want milk.

GRUSHA (*giving the child some milk*). This is an expensive joke. Take a sip, Michael, it's a week's pay. The people here think we earned our money just sitting around. Michael, Michael, you're a nice little load for anyone to take on! (*Uneasy, she gets up, puts the child on her back, and walks on. The Old Man, grumbling, picks up the pitcher and looks after her unmoved.*)

THE STORY TELLER.
As Grusha Vashnadze went northward
The Princes' Ironshirts went after her.

THE CHORUS.
How will the barefoot girl escape the Ironshirts,
The bloodhounds, the trap-setters?
They are hunting even by night.
Pursuers never get tired.
Butchers sleep little.

(*Two Ironshirts are trudging along the highway.*)

THE CORPORAL. You'll never amount to anything, blockhead!

Your heart's not in it. Your senior officer sees it in little things. Yesterday, when I made the fat gal, I admit you grabbed her husband as I commanded, and you *did* kick him in the stomach, but did you enjoy doing it like a loyal Private? Or were you just doing your duty? I've kept my eyes on you, blockhead. You're a hollow reed and a tinkling cymbal. You won't get promoted. (*They walk a while in silence.*) Don't imagine I don't remember how insubordinate you are in everything. I forbid you to limp! You only do it because I sold the horses, and I sold 'em because I couldn't have got that price again. You limp just to show me you don't like marching. I know you. It won't help. You wait. Sing!

THE TWO IRONSHIRTS (*singing*).

    Off to the wars I went my way
    Leaving my loved one at her door
    My friends will keep her honor safe
    Till from the wars I'm back once more.

THE CORPORAL. Louder!

THE TWO IRONSHIRTS (*singing*).

    And when my heavenly rest is won
    My love will at my grave declare:
    "Here rest the feet that once to me would run
    And here the hands that once caressed my hair!"

(*They begin to walk again in silence.*)

THE CORPORAL. A good soldier has his heart and soul in it. When he receives an order, he gets a hard on, and when he sends his lance into the enemy's guts, he comes. (*He shouts for joy.*) He lets himself be torn to pieces for his superior officer, and as he lies dying he takes note that his corporal is nodding approval. That's reward enough for him. That's all he wants. But *you* won't get a nod. Yet you'll croak all the same. Christ, how am I to get my hands on the Governor's bastard with a fool like you! (*They stay on stage behind.*)

THE STORY TELLER.

    When Grusha Vashnadze came to the River Sirra
    The flight grew too much for her, the helpless child
      too heavy.

128

In the cornfields the rosy dawn
Is cold to the sleepless one, only cold.
The gay clatter of the milk cans in the farmyard
      where the smoke rises
Is only a threat to the fugitive.
She who carries the child feels its weight and
      little more.

(*Grusha stops in front of a farm. A fat peasant woman is carrying a milk can through the door. Grusha waits until she has gone in, then approaches the house cautiously.*)

GRUSHA (*to the child*). Now you've wet yourself again, and you know I've no linen. Michael, this is where we part company. This is far enough from the city. They wouldn't want you so much, little good-for-nothing, that they'd follow you all this way. The woman is kind, and can't you just smell the milk? (*She bends down to lay the child on the threshold.*) So farewell, Michael, I will forget how you kicked me in the back all night to make me go faster. And you, forget the meager fare — it was meant well. I would like to have kept you — your nose is so tiny — but it cannot be. I would have shown you your first rabbit and how not to wet yourself, but I must turn back. My sweetheart the soldier might soon return. And suppose he didn't find me? You can't ask that. (*She creeps up to the door and lays the child on the threshold. Then, hiding behind a tree, she waits until the peasant woman opens the door and sees the bundle.*)

THE PEASANT WOMAN. Good heavens, what's that? Husband!

THE PEASANT (*coming*). What's up? Let me get on with my soup.

THE PEASANT WOMAN (*to the child*). Where's your mother then? Haven't you got one? It's a boy. Fine linen — and a child. From a good family, you can see that. And they just leave him on our doorstep. Oh, these are times!

THE PEASANT. If they think we're going to feed it, they're mistaken. You can take it to the priest in the village. That's the best we can do.

THE PEASANT WOMAN. What will the priest do with it? It needs

129

a mother. There, it's waking up. Don't you think we could keep it though?

THE PEASANT (*shouting*). No!

THE PEASANT WOMAN. I could lay it in the corner next to the armchair. I only need a crib for it. And I can take it into the fields with me. See how it's laughing? Husband, we have a roof over our heads and we can do it. I won't hear any more. (*She carries the child into the house. The Peasant follows, protesting. Grusha steps out from behind the tree, laughs, and hurries off in the opposite direction.*)

THE STORY TELLER. Why so cheerful, making for home?

THE CHORUS.   Because the child has won new parents
                        with a laugh,
                 Because I'm rid of the little one, I'm
                        cheerful.

THE STORY TELLER. And why so sad?

THE CHORUS.   Because I'm single and free, I'm sad.
                 Like one robbed, one newly poor.

(*She walks for a short while, then meets the two Ironshirts, who point their lances at her.*)

THE CORPORAL. Lady, you are running into the Armed Forces. Where are you coming from? And when? Are you entertaining illicit relations with the enemy? Where is he hiding? What sort of movements is he making in your rear? What about the hills? What about the valley? How are the stockings fastened? (*Grusha stands there frightened.*) Don't be scared, we always stage retreats, if necessary . . . what, blockhead? I always stage retreats. In that respect, I'm reliable. Why are you staring like that at the lance? In the field no soldier ever drops his lance, that's a rule. Learn it by heart, blockhead. Now then, lady, where are you heading for?

GRUSHA. To meet my intended, one Simon Shashava, of the Palace Guard in Nuka.

THE CORPORAL. Simon Shashava? Sure, I know *him*. He gave me the key so I could look you up once in a while. Blockhead, we are getting unpopular. We must make her realize we have honorable intentions. Lady, behind apparent frivolity I conceal a serious nature. And so I'll tell you officially: I want a child from you. (*Grusha utters a little scream.*) Blockhead, she's understood. Uh-huh, isn't it a sweet shock? "Then first I must take the noodles out of the oven, Officer. Then first I must change my torn shirt, Colonel." But away with jokes, away with the lance! We are looking for a child in these parts. A child from a good family. Have you heard of such a child, from the city, dressed in fine linen, and suddenly turning up here?

GRUSHA. No, I haven't heard a thing. (*Suddenly she turns round and runs back, panic-stricken. The Ironshirts glance at each other, then follow her, cursing.*)

THE STORY TELLER. Run, kind girl! The killers are coming!
Help the helpless child, helpless girl!
And so she runs!

THE CHORUS. In the bloodiest times
There are kind people.

(*As Grusha rushes into the cottage, the Peasant Woman is bending over the child's crib.*)

GRUSHA. Hide it! Quick! The Ironshirts are coming! It was I who laid it on your doorstep. But it isn't mine. It's from a good family.

THE PEASANT WOMAN. Who's coming? What sort of Ironshirts?

GRUSHA. Don't ask questions. The Ironshirts that are looking for it.

THE PEASANT WOMAN. They've no business in my house. But I must have a little talk with *you*, it seems.

GRUSHA. Take off the fine linen. That will give us away.

THE PEASANT WOMAN. Linen here, linen there. In this house *I* make the decisions. *You* can't vomit in *my* room! But why did you abandon it? That's a sin.

GRUSHA (*looking out of the window*). There, they're coming from behind the trees. I shouldn't have run away. That made them angry. Oh, what shall I do?

THE PEASANT WOMAN (*looking out of the window and suddenly starting with fear*). Good gracious! Ironshirts!

131

GRUSHA. They're after the child!

THE PEASANT WOMAN. But suppose they come in!

GRUSHA. You musn't give it to them. Say it's yours.

THE PEASANT WOMAN. Yes.

GRUSHA. They'll run it through if you hand it over.

THE PEASANT WOMAN. But suppose they ask for it? The silver for the harvest is in the house.

GRUSHA. If you let them have it, they'll run it through, here in your room! You've got to say it's yours!

THE PEASANT WOMAN. Yes. But what if they don't believe me?

GRUSHA. You must speak firmly.

THE PEASANT WOMAN. They'll burn the roof over our head.

GRUSHA. That's why you've got to say it's yours. His name's Michael. I shouldn't have told you that. (*The Peasant Woman nods.*) Don't nod like that with your head. And don't tremble — they'll notice.

THE PEASANT WOMAN. Yes.

GRUSHA. Stop saying yes. I can't stand it any longer. (*She shakes the woman.*) Haven't *you* got a child?

THE PEASANT WOMAN (*muttering*). In the war.

GRUSHA. Then maybe he's an Ironshirt too? Do you want him to run children through with his lance? You'd bawl him out. "Stop fooling with a lance in my house!" you'd shout, "is that what I've reared you for? Wash your neck before you speak to your mother!"

THE PEASANT WOMAN. That's true, he couldn't do that around here!

GRUSHA. Promise me you'll say it's yours.

THE PEASANT WOMAN. Yes.

GRUSHA. There! They're coming now!

(*There is a knocking at the door. The women don't answer. Enter Ironshirts. The Peasant Woman bows low.*)

THE CORPORAL. Well, there she is. What did I tell you? What a nose I have! I smell her. Lady, I have to ask you a question. Why did you run away? What did you think I would do to you? I'll bet it was something dirty. Confess!

GRUSHA (*while the Peasant Woman bows again and again*). I'd left the milk on the stove, and I suddenly remembered it.

THE CORPORAL. Or maybe you imagined I'd looked at you in a dirty way? As if I thought there could be something between us? A lewd look, know what I mean?

GRUSHA. I didn't see it.

THE CORPORAL. But it's possible, huh? You admit that. After all, I might be a swine. I'm quite frank with you. I could think of all sorts of things if we were alone. (*To the Peasant Woman*) Shouldn't you be busy in the yard? Feeding the hens?

THE PEASANT WOMAN (*falling suddenly to her knees*). Soldier, I didn't know a thing about it. Please don't burn the roof over our heads.

THE CORPORAL. What are you talking about?

THE PEASANT WOMAN. I have nothing to do with it. She left it on my doorstep, I swear it.

THE CORPORAL (*suddenly seeing the child and whistling*). Ah, there's a little something in the crib! Blockhead, I smell a thousand piasters. Take the old girl out and hold on to her. It looks as though I'll have to do some cross-examining. (*The Peasant Woman lets herself be led out by the Private, without a word.*) Well, you've got the child I wanted from you. (*He walks toward the crib.*)

GRUSHA. Officer, it's mine. It's not the one you're looking for.

THE CORPORAL. I'll just have a look at it. (*He bends over the crib. Grusha looks round in despair.*)

GRUSHA. It's mine! It's mine!

THE CORPORAL. Fine linen!

(*Grusha dashes at him to pull him away. He throws her off and again bends over the crib. Again looking round in despair, she sees a log of wood, seizes it, and hits the Corporal over the head from behind. The Corporal collapses. She quickly picks up the child and rushes off.*)

THE STORY TELLER.

> And in her flight from the Ironshirts
> After twenty-two days of journeying
> At the foot of the Janga-Tu glacier
> Grusha Vashnadze decided to adopt the child.

133

THE CHORUS.

The helpless girl adopted the helpless child.

(Grusha squats over a half-frozen stream to get the child water in the hollow of her hand.)

GRUSHA. Since no one wants to take you
      I must take you now
      And, as there is no one else,
      (O black day in a meager year!)
      You must be content with me.
      Since I've carried you too long
      And with sore feet
      Since the milk was too dear
      I grew fond of you.
      (I wouldn't be without you any more.)
      I'll throw your fine shirt away
      And wrap you up in rags
      I'll wash you and christen you
      With glacier water
      (You must see it through).

(She has taken off the child's fine linen and wrapped it in a rag.)

THE STORY TELLER.

      When Grusha Vashnadze
      Pursued by the Ironshirts
      Came to the bridge on the glacier
      Leading to the villages of the Eastern Slope
      She sang the Song of the Rotten Bridge
      And risked two lives.

(A wind has risen. The bridge on the glacier is visible in the dark. One rope is broken and half the bridge is hanging down the abyss. Merchants, two men and a woman, stand undecided before the bridge as Grusha and the child arrive. One man is trying to catch the hanging rope with a stick.)

THE FIRST MAN. Take your time, young woman. You won't get over that pass anyway.

GRUSHA. But I simply have to get the little one over to the east side. To my brother.

THE MERCHANT WOMAN. Have to? What d'you mean by "have to"? I have to get there, too — because I have to buy two carpets in Atum — carpets a woman had to sell because her husband had to die. But can I do what I have to? Can she? For hours Andréi has been fishing for that rope. And I ask you, how are we to fasten it, even if he gets it up?

THE FIRST MAN (*listening*). Hush, I think I hear something.

GRUSHA. The bridge is not quite rotten. I think I'll try and make it.

THE MERCHANT WOMAN. I wouldn't try that even if the devil himself were after me. Why it's suicide.

THE FIRST MAN (*shouting*). Hi!

GRUSHA. Don't call! (*To the Merchant Woman*) Tell him not to call.

THE FIRST MAN. But there's someone down there calling. Maybe they've lost their way.

THE MERCHANT WOMAN. Why shouldn't he call? Is there something wrong about you? Are they after you?

GRUSHA. Well, I'll tell you. The Ironshirts are after me. I knocked one down.

THE SECOND MAN. Hide our merchandise!

(*The Woman hides a sack behind a rock.*)

THE FIRST MAN. Why didn't you tell us that right away? (*To the others*) If they catch her they'll make mincemeat out of her!

GRUSHA. Get out of my way. I've got to cross that bridge.

THE SECOND MAN. You can't. The precipice is two thousand feet deep.

THE FIRST MAN. Even with the rope it'd be no use. We could hold it with our hands, but then the Ironshirts could cross the same way.

GRUSHA. Go away.

(*There are calls from the distance*: "Hi, up there!")

THE MERCHANT WOMAN. They're getting near. But you can't take the child across that bridge. It's sure to break. Just look down!

(*Grusha looks down into the abyss. The Ironshirts are heard calling again from below.*)

135

THE SECOND MAN. Two thousand feet!

GRUSHA. But those men are worse.

THE FIRST MAN. You can't do it. There's the child. Risk *your* life but not the child's.

THE SECOND MAN. With the child she's all the heavier!

THE MERCHANT WOMAN. Maybe she's really got to get across. Give me the child. I'll hide it. You cross the bridge alone.

GRUSHA. I won't. We belong together. (*To the child*) "Live together, die together." (*She sings.*)

THE SONG OF THE ROTTEN BRIDGE

Deep is the abyss, son,
I see the weak bridge sway
But it's not for us, son,
To choose the way.

The way I know
Is the one you must tread,
And all you will eat
Is my bit of bread.

Of every four pieces
You shall have three.
I wish I knew
How big they will be!

Get out of my way, I'll try it without the rope.

THE MERCHANT WOMAN. That's tempting God!

(*There are shouts from below.*)

GRUSHA. I beg you, throw that stick away, or they'll get the rope and follow me. (*Pressing the child to her, she steps onto the swaying bridge. The Merchant Woman screams when it looks as though the bridge is about to collapse. But Grusha walks on and reaches the far side.*)

THE FIRST MAN. She's done it!

THE MERCHANT WOMAN (*who has fallen on her knees and begun to pray, angrily*). I still think it was a sin.

(*The Ironshirts appear; the Corporal's head is bandaged.*)

THE CORPORAL. Have you seen a woman with a child?

THE FIRST MAN (*while the Second Man throws the stick into the abyss*). Yes, there she is! But the bridge won't carry *you*!

THE CORPORAL. You'll have to pay for this, blockhead!

(*Grusha, from the far bank, laughs and shows the child to the Ironshirts. She walks on. The wind blows.*)

GRUSHA (*turning to the child*). You mustn't fear the wind. He's just a poor thing too. He has to push the clouds along and he gets cold doing it. (*Snow starts falling.*) And the snow is not so bad, either, Michael. It covers the little fir trees so they won't die in winter. And now I'll sing you a little song. Listen! (*She sings.*)

THE SONG OF THE CHILD
Your father is a thief,
Your mother is a whore,
And all good people
Will kneel at your door.

The sons of the tiger
Are the horse's brothers,
The child of the snake
Brings milk to the mothers.

3

IN THE NORTHERN MOUNTAINS

THE STORY TELLER.
Seven days the sister, Grusha Vashnadze,
Journeyed across the glacier
And down the slopes she journeyed.
"When I enter my brother's house," she thought

137

"He will rise and embrace me."
"Is that you, sister?" he will say,
"I have been expecting you so long.
This is my dear wife.
And this is my farm, come to me by marriage,
With eleven horses and thirty-one cows. Sit down.
Sit down with your child at our table and eat."
The brother's house was in a lovely valley.
When the sister came to the brother,
She was ill from walking.
The brother rose from the table.

(*A fat peasant couple rise from the table. Lavrenti Vash-nadze still has a napkin round his neck, as Grusha, pale and supported by a servant, enters with the child.*)

LAVRENTI. Where do you come from, Grusha?

GRUSHA (*feebly*). I've walked across the Janga-Tu Pass, Lavrenti.

THE SERVANT. I found her in front of the hay barn. She has a child with her.

THE SISTER-IN-LAW. Go and groom the mare. (*Exit the Servant.*)

LAVRENTI. This is my wife, Aniko.

THE SISTER-IN-LAW. I thought you were in service in Nuka.

GRUSHA (*barely able to stand*). Yes, I was there.

THE SISTER-IN-LAW. Wasn't it a good job? We were told it was so good.

GRUSHA. The Governor has been killed.

LAVRENTI. Yes, we heard there were riots. Your aunt told us about it. Remember, Aniko?

THE SISTER-IN-LAW. Here, with us, it's very quiet. City people always want something going on. (*She walks toward the door, calling*) Sosso, Sosso, don't take the cake out of the oven yet, d'you hear? Where on earth are you? (*Exit, calling.*)

LAVRENTI (*quietly, quickly*). Is there a father? (*As she shakes her head*) I thought not. We must think up something. She's religious.

THE SISTER-IN-LAW (*returning*). Those servants! (*To Grusha*) You have a child.

GRUSHA. It's mine. (*She collapses. Lavrenti rushes to her assistance.*)

THE SISTER-IN-LAW. Good heavens, she's ill — what are we to do?

LAVRENTI (*escorting her to a bench near the stove*). Sit down, sit down. I think it's just weakness, Aniko.

THE SISTER-IN-LAW. As long as it's not scarlet fever!

LAVRENTI. Then she'd have spots. It's only weakness. Don't worry, Aniko. (*To Grusha*) It's better sitting down?

THE SISTER-IN-LAW. Is the child hers?

GRUSHA. It's mine.

LAVRENTI. She's on her way to her husband.

THE SISTER-IN-LAW. I see. Your meat's getting cold. (*Lavrenti sits down and begins to eat.*) Cold food's not good for you, the fat mustn't get cold, you know your stomach's your weak spot. (*To Grusha*) If your husband's not in the city, where is he?

LAVRENTI. She got married on the other side of the mountain, she says.

THE SISTER-IN-LAW. Oh, on the other side. (*She also sits down to eat.*)

GRUSHA. I think I should lie down somewhere, Lavrenti.

THE SISTER-IN-LAW. If it's consumption we'll all get it. (*She goes on cross-examining her.*) Has your husband a farm?

GRUSHA. He's a soldier.

LAVRENTI. But he's coming into a farm — a small one from his father.

THE SISTER-IN-LAW. Isn't he in the war? Why not?

GRUSHA (*with effort*). Yes, he's in the war.

THE SISTER-IN-LAW. Then why d'you want to go to the farm?

LAVRENTI. When he comes back from the war, he'll come to his farm.

THE SISTER-IN-LAW. But you're going there now?

LAVRENTI. Yes, to wait for him.

THE SISTER-IN-LAW (*calling shrilly*). Sosso, the cake!

139

GRUSHA (*murmuring feverishly*). A farm — a soldier — waiting — sit down, eat.

THE SISTER-IN-LAW. It's scarlet fever.

GRUSHA (*starting up*). Yes, he has a farm!

LAVRENTI. I think it's just weakness, Aniko. Wouldn't you like to go and look after the cake yourself, dear?

THE SISTER-IN-LAW. But when will he come back if war has broken out again as people say? (*She waddles off, shouting.*) Sosso! where on earth are you? Sosso!

LAVRENTI (*getting up quickly and going to Grusha*). You'll get a bed in a minute. She has a good heart. But wait till after supper.

GRUSHA (*holding out the child to him*). Take him.

LAVRENTI (*taking it and looking around*). But you can't stay here long with the child. She's religious, you see. (*Grusha collapses. Lavrenti catches her.*)

THE STORY TELLER.

> The sister was so ill,
> The cowardly brother had to give her shelter.
> Summer departed, winter came.
> The winter was long, the winter was short:
> People mustn't know anything,
> The rats mustn't bite,
> The spring mustn't come.

(*Grusha sits over the weaving loom in a workroom. She and the child, who is squatting on the floor, are wrapped in blankets. She sings.*)

THE SONG OF THE WAR'S CENTER

> And the lover started to leave
> And his betrothed ran pleading after him
> Pleading and weeping, weeping and teaching:
> "Dearest mine, Dearest mine
> As now you go to the war
> As now you are to fight the enemy
> Don't throw yourself into the front line
> And don't push with the rear line

In front is red fire
In the rear is red smoke
Stay in the war's center
Stay near the standard bearer
The first ones always die
The last ones are also hit
Those in the center come home."

Michael, we must be clever. If we make ourselves as small as cockroaches, the sister-in-law will forget we are in the house. Then we can stay here till the snow melts.

(*Enter Lavrenti. He sits down beside his sister.*)

LAVRENTI. Why are you two sitting there muffled up like coachmen? Is it too cold in the room?

GRUSHA (*hastily removing one shawl*). It's not too cold, Lavrenti.

LAVRENTI. If it's too cold, you oughtn't to sit here with the child. Aniko would think herself to blame. (*pause*) I hope our priest didn't question you about the child?

GRUSHA. He did, but I didn't tell him anything.

LAVRENTI. That's good. I wanted to talk to you about Aniko. She has a good heart but she's very very sensitive. People have only to mention our farm and she's worried. She takes everything so hard, you see. One time our milkmaid went to church with a hole in her stocking. Ever since that day my Aniko has worn two pairs of stockings at church. It may seem hard to believe, but it's the old family in her. (*He listens.*) Are you sure there are no rats around? If so, you couldn't live here. (*There are sounds as of dripping from the roof.*) What's that dripping?

GRUSHA. It must be a barrel leaking.

LAVRENTI. Yes, it must be a barrel. You've been here half a year now, haven't you? Was I talking about Aniko? (*They listen again to the snow melting.*) You can't imagine how worried she is about your soldier-husband. "Supposing he comes back and doesn't find her!" she says and lies awake. "He can't come before the Spring," I tell her. The dear woman! (*The drops begin to fall faster.*) When d'you think

141

he'll come? What do *you* think? (*Grusha is silent.*) Not before the spring, you think that too? (*Grusha is silent.*) So now you don't believe he'll come back at all? (*Grusha is silent.*) But when the Spring comes and the snow is melting here and on the passes, you can't stay any longer. They may come and look for you. The people are already beginning to talk about an illegitimate child. (*The "glockenspiel" of the falling drops has grown faster and steadier.*) Grusha, the snow is melting on the roof. And spring is here.

GRUSHA. Yes.

LAVRENTI (*eagerly*). Let me tell you what we'll do. You need a place to go, and because of the child (*he sighs*) you have to have a husband so people won't talk. Now I've made cautious inquiries to see if we can get a husband for you. Grusha, I've found one. I talked to a woman who has a son. Just the other side of the mountain, a small farm. She's willing.

GRUSHA. But I can't marry anyone! I must wait for Simon Shashava.

LAVRENTI. Of course. That's all been taken care of. You don't need a man in bed — you *do* need a man on paper. And I've found you one. The son of that peasant woman is just going to die. Isn't it wonderful? He's at the last gasp. And everything's as we said it was. A husband from the other side of the mountain. When you met him he was at the last gasp. And so you're a widow. What do you say?

GRUSHA. I could do with a document with stamps on it for Michael.

LAVRENTI. The stamps make all the difference. Without something in writing the Shah of Persia couldn't prove he's it. And you'll have a place to live.

GRUSHA. How much does the woman want for it?

LAVRENTI. Four hundred piasters.

GRUSHA. Where will you get the money from?

LAVRENTI (*guiltily*). Aniko's milk money.

GRUSHA. No one would know us there. I'll do it.

LAVRENTI (*getting up*). I'll let the peasant woman know right now. (*Quick exit.*)

142

GRUSHA. Michael, you cause a lot of fuss. I came to you as the pear tree comes to the sparrows. And because a Christian bends down and picks up a crust of bread so nothing will go to waste. Michael, it would have been better had I walked quickly away on that Easter Sunday in Nuka in the second courtyard. Now I *am* a fool.

THE STORY TELLER.

> The bridegroom was lying on his deathbed when
> the bride arrived.
> The bridegroom's mother was waiting at the door,
> telling her to hurry.
> The bride brought a child along.
> The witness hid it during the wedding.

(*On one side the bed. Under the mosquito net lies a very sick man. Grusha is pulled in at a run by her future mother-in-law. They are followed by Lavrenti and the child.*)

THE MOTHER-IN-LAW. Quick! Quick! Or he'll die on us before the wedding. (*To Lavrenti*) I was never told she had a child already.

LAVRENTI. What difference does it make? (*Pointing toward the dying man*) It can't matter to him — in his condition.

THE MOTHER-IN-LAW. To him? But I won't survive the shame. We are honest people. (*She begins to weep.*) My Jussup doesn't have to marry a girl with a child!

LAVRENTI. All right, I'll give you another two hundred piasters. You have it in writing that the farm will go to you. But she has the right to live here for two years.

THE MOTHER-IN-LAW (*drying her tears*). It'll hardly cover the funeral expenses. I hope she'll really lend me a hand with the work. And now what's happened to the monk? He must have crept out through the kitchen window. We'll have the whole village round our necks when they get wind that Jussup's end has come! Oh dear! I'll run and bring the monk. But he mustn't see the child.

LAVRENTI. I'll take care he doesn't see it. But why only a monk? Why not a priest?

THE MOTHER-IN-LAW. Oh, he's just as good. I only made one

143

mistake: I paid him half his fee in advance. Enough to go to the tavern with. I only hope . . . (*She runs off.*)

LAVRENTI. She saved on the priest, the wretch! Hired a cheap monk.

GRUSHA. Send Simon Shashava over to see me if he turns up after all.

LAVRENTI. Yes. (*Pointing at the sick man*) Won't you have a look at him? (*Grusha, taking Michael to her, shakes her head.*) He's not moving an eyelid. I hope we aren't too late. (*They listen. On the opposite side enter neighbors who look around and take up positions against the walls, thus forming another wall near the bed, yet leaving an opening so that the bed can be seen. They start murmuring prayers. Enter the Mother-in-law with a monk. Showing some annoyance and surprise, she bows to the guests.*)

THE MOTHER-IN-LAW. If you don't mind, please wait a few moments. My son's bride has just arrived from the city and an emergency wedding is about to take place. (*To the Monk in the bedroom*) I might have known you'd blue it in. (*To Grusha*) The wedding can take place immediately. Here's the license. I and the bride's brother (*Lavrenti tries to hide in the background, after having quietly taken Michael back from Grusha. The Mother-in-law waves him away*) who will appear at once, are the witnesses.

(*Grusha has bowed to the Monk. They go to the bed. The Mother-in-law lifts the mosquito net. The Monk starts reeling off the marriage ceremony in Latin. Meanwhile, the Mother-in-law beckons to Lavrenti to get rid of the child, but fearing that it will cry he draws its attention to the ceremony. Grusha glances once at the child, and Lavrenti waves the child's hand in a greeting.*)

THE MONK. Are you prepared to be a faithful, obedient, and good wife to this man, and to cleave to him until death you do part?

GRUSHA (*looking at the child*). I am.

THE MONK (*to the sick peasant*). And are you prepared to be a good and loving husband to your wife until death you do part? (*As the sick peasant does not answer, the Monk looks inquiringly around.*)

THE MOTHER-IN-LAW. Of course he is! Didn't you hear him say yes?

THE MONK. All right. We declare the marriage contracted! Now what about Extreme Unction?

THE MOTHER-IN-LAW. Nothing doing! The wedding was quite expensive enough. Now I must take care of the mourners. (*To Lavrenti*) Did we say seven hundred?

LAVRENTI. Six hundred. (*He pays.*) Now I don't want to sit with the guests and get to know people. So farewell, Grusha. And if my widowed sister comes to visit me one day, she'll get a welcome from my wife, or I'll get disagreeable.

(*Lavrenti nods, gives the child to Grusha, and leaves. The mourners glance after him without interest.*)

THE MONK. And may one ask where this child comes from?

THE MOTHER-IN-LAW. Is there a child? I don't see a child. And you don't see one either — you understand? Or else, I shall have seen all kinds of things in the tavern! Now come on. (*After Grusha has put the child down and told him to be quiet, they move over left. Grusha is introduced to the neighbors.*) This is my daughter-in-law. She arrived just in time to find dear Jussup still alive.

ONE WOMAN. He's been ill now a whole year, hasn't he? When our Vassili was drafted he was there to say goodbye.

ANOTHER WOMAN. Such things are terrible for a farm. The corn all ripe and the farmer in bed! It'll really be a blessing if he doesn't suffer too long, I say.

THE FIRST WOMAN (*confidentially*). At first we thought it was because of the draft he'd taken to his bed, you know. And now his end is coming!

THE MOTHER-IN-LAW. Sit yourselves down, please, and have some cakes. (*She beckons to Grusha and both women go into the bedroom, where they pick up the cake pans off the floor. The guests, among them the Monk, sit on the floor and begin conversing in subdued voices.*)

145

ONE PEASANT (*to whom the Monk has handed the bottle which he has taken from his soutane*). There's a child, you say! How can that have happened to Jussup?

A WOMAN. She was certainly lucky to get herself hitched, with him so sick.

THE MOTHER-IN-LAW. They're gossiping already. And gorging on the funeral cakes at the same time! If he doesn't die today, I'll have to bake fresh ones tomorrow.

GRUSHA. I'll bake them.

THE MOTHER-IN-LAW. Yesterday the horsemen rode by, and I went out to see who it was. When I came in again he was lying there like a corpse! That's why I sent for you. It can't take much longer. (*She listens.*)

THE MONK. My dear wedding and funeral guests! Deeply touched, we stand before a bed of death and marriage. The bride gets the veil; the groom, a shroud: how varied, my children, are the fates of men! Alas! One man dies and has a roof over his head, and the other is married and the flesh turns to dust, from which it was made. Amen.

THE MOTHER-IN-LAW. He's taking his revenge. I shouldn't have hired such a cheap one. It's what you'd expect. A more expensive one would behave himself. In Sura there's one with a real air of sanctity about him, but of course he charges a fortune. A fifty-piaster monk like that has no dignity. And as for piety, just fifty piasters' worth and no more! When I came to get him in the tavern he had just made a speech and was shouting: "The war is over, beware of the peace!" We must go in.

GRUSHA (*giving Michael a cake*). Eat this cake, and keep nice and still, Michael.

(*The two women offer cakes to the guests. The dying man sits up in bed. He puts his head out from under the mosquito net, stares at the two women, then sinks back again. The Monk takes two bottles from his soutane and offers them to the peasant beside him. Enter three musicians who are greeted with a sly wink by the Monk.*)

THE MOTHER-IN-LAW (*to the musicians*). What are you doing here? With instruments?

ONE MUSICIAN. Brother Anastasius here (*pointing at the Monk*) told us there was a wedding going on.

THE MOTHER-IN-LAW. What? *You* brought them? Three more on my neck! Don't you know there's a dying man in the next room?

THE MONK. A very tempting assignment for an artist: something that could be either a subdued Wedding March or a spirited Funeral Dance!

THE MOTHER-IN-LAW. Well, you might as well play. Nobody can stop you eating in any case.

(*The musicians play a potpourri. The women serve cakes.*)

THE MONK. The trumpet sounds like a whining baby. And you, little drum, what have you got to tell the world?

THE DRUNKEN PEASANT (*beside the Monk, sings*).

Miss Roundass took the old old man
And said that marriage was the thing
　　To everyone who met 'er.
She later withdrew from the contract because
　　Candles are better.

(*The Mother-in-law leads the Drunken Peasant out. The music stops. The guests are embarrassed.*)

THE GUESTS (*loudly*). Have you heard? The Grand Duke is back! But the Princes are against him.

— Oh, the Shah of Persia, they say, has lent him a great army, to restore order in Grusinia. How is this possible? After all, the Shah of Persia is the enemy . . .

— Only the enemy of Grusinia, you ass, not of the Grand Duke!

— In any case, the war's over, our soldiers are coming back.

(*Grusha drops a cake pan. Guests help her pick up the cake.*)

AN OLD WOMAN (*to Grusha*). Are you feeling bad? That's just excitement about dear Jussup. Sit down and rest awhile, my dear.

(*Grusha staggers.*)

THE GUESTS. Now everything will be as it was. Only the taxes'll go up because we'll have to pay for the war.

GRUSHA (*weakly*). Did someone say the soldiers are back?

A MAN. I did.

GRUSHA. It can't be true.

THE FIRST MAN (*to a woman*). Show her the shawl. We bought it from a soldier. It's from Persia.

GRUSHA (*looking at the shawl*). They are here. (*She gets up, takes a step, kneels down in prayer, takes the silver cross and chain out of her blouse, and kisses it.*)

THE MOTHER-IN-LAW (*while the guests silently watch Grusha*). What's the matter with you? Won't you look after our guests? What's all this nonsense from the city got to do with us?

THE GUESTS (*resuming conversation while Grusha remains in prayer*). You can buy Persian saddles from the soldiers too. Though some exchange them for crutches.

— The big shots on one side can win a war, but the soldiers on both sides lose it.

— Anyway, the war's over now. It's something that they can't draft you anymore. (*The dying man sits bolt upright in bed. He listens.*) What we need is two weeks of good weather.

— Our pear trees are hardly bearing a thing this year.

THE MOTHER-IN-LAW (*offering cakes*). Have some more cake and enjoy it. There are more. (*The Mother-in-law goes to the bedroom with the empty cake pans. Unaware of the dying man, she is bending down to pick up another tray when he begins to talk in a hoarse voice.*)

THE PEASANT. How many cakes are you going to stuff down· their throats? D'you think I can *shit* money? (*The Mother-in-law starts, stares at him aghast, while he climbs out from behind the mosquito net.*)

THE FIRST WOMAN (*talking kindly to Grusha in the next room*). Has the young wife someone at the front?

A MAN. That's good news, they're on their way home, huh?

THE PEASANT. Don't stare like that! Where's this wife you've hung round my neck?

(*Receiving no answer, he climbs out of bed and in his night-shirt staggers into the other room. Trembling, she follows him with the cake pan.*)

THE GUESTS (*seeing him and shrieking*). Good God! Jussup! (*Everyone leaps up in alarm. The women rush to the door. Grusha, still on her knees, turns round and stares at the man.*)

THE PEASANT. The funeral supper! *That's* what you would like! Get out before I throw you out! (*As the guests stampede from the house, gloomily to Grusha*) I've upset the apple cart, huh? (*Receiving no answer, he turns round and takes a cake from the pan which his mother is holding.*)

THE STORY TELLER.

O confusion! The wife discovers she has a husband.
By day there's the child, by night there's
   the husband.
The lover is on his way both day and night.
Husband and wife look at each other.
The bedroom is small.

(*Near the bed the Peasant is sitting in a high wooden bathtub, naked. The Mother-in-law is pouring water from a pitcher. Opposite, Grusha cowers with Michael, who is playing at mending a straw hat.*)

THE PEASANT (*to his mother*). That's *her* work, not yours. Where's she hiding out now?

THE MOTHER-IN-LAW (*calling*). Grusha! The peasant wants you!

GRUSHA (*to Michael*). There are still two holes to mend.

THE PEASANT (*when Grusha approaches*). Scrub my back!

GRUSHA. Can't the peasant do it himself?

THE PEASANT. "Can't the peasant do it himself?" Get the brush! To hell with you! Are you the wife here? Or are you a visitor? (*To the Mother-in-law*) It's too cold!

THE MOTHER-IN-LAW. I'll run for hot water.

GRUSHA. Let me go.

THE PEASANT. You stay here. (*The Mother-in-law runs.*) Rub harder. And no finagling. You've seen a naked fellow before. That child didn't come out of thin air.

GRUSHA. The child was not conceived in joy, if that's what the peasant means.

THE PEASANT (*turning and grinning*). You don't look the type.

149

(*Grusha stops scrubbing him, starts back. Enter the Mother-in-law.*) A nice thing you've hung around my neck! A simpleton for a wife!

THE MOTHER-IN-LAW. She just isn't cooperative.

THE PEASANT. Pour—but go easy! Ow! Go easy, I said. (*To Grusha*) Maybe you did something wrong in the city . . . I wouldn't be surprised. Why else should you be here? But I won't talk about that. I've not said a word about the illegitimate object you brought into my house either. But my patience has limits! It's against nature. (*To the Mother-in-law*) More! (*To Grusha*) And even if your soldier does come back, you're married.

GRUSHA. Yes.

THE PEASANT. But your soldier won't return now. Don't you believe it.

GRUSHA. No.

THE PEASANT. You're cheating me. You're my wife and you're not my wife. Where you lie, nothing lies, and yet no other woman can lie there. When I go to work in the mornings I'm dead tired — when I lie down at night I'm awake as the devil. God has given you sex — and what d'you do? I don't have ten piasters to buy myself a woman in the city! Besides, it's a long way. Woman weeds the fields and opens up her legs, that's what our calendar says. D'you hear?

GRUSHA (*quietly*). Yes. I don't wish to cheat you out of it.

THE PEASANT. She doesn't wish to cheat me out of it! Pour some more water! (*The Mother-in-law pours.*) Ow!

THE STORY TELLER.
As she sat by the stream to wash the linen
She saw his image in the water,
And his face grew dimmer with the passing moons.
As she raised herself to wring the linen
She heard his voice from the murmuring maple
And his voice grew fainter with the passing moons.
Evasions and sighs grew more numerous,
Tears and sweat flowed.
With the passing moons the child grew up.

(*Grusha sits by a stream, dipping linen into the water. In the rear, a few children are standing.*)

GRUSHA (*to Michael*). You can play with them, Michael, but don't let them order you about just because you're the smallest. (*Michael nods and joins the children. They start playing.*)

THE BIGGEST BOY. Today we're going to play Heads-Off. (*To a Fat Boy*) You're the Prince and you must laugh. (*To Michael*) You're the Governor, and you laugh. (*To a Girl*) You're the Governor's wife and you cry when his head's chopped off. And I do the chopping. (*He shows his wooden sword.*) With this. First, the Governor is led into the yard. The Prince walks ahead. The Governor's wife comes last. (*They form a procession. The Fat Boy goes ahead and laughs. Then comes Michael, then the Biggest Boy, and then the Girl, who weeps.*)

MICHAEL (*standing still*). Me too chop head off.

THE BIGGEST BOY. That's my job. You're the smallest. The Governor's part is the easiest. All you have to do is kneel down and have your head chopped off — very simple.

MICHAEL. Me too have sword.

THE BIGGEST BOY. That's mine. (*He gives him a kick.*)

THE GIRL (*shouting to Grusha*). He doesn't want to play.

GRUSHA (*laughing*). Even the *little* duck can swim, they say.

THE BIGGEST BOY. You can play the Prince if you know how to laugh. (*Michael shakes his head.*)

THE FAT BOY. I laugh best. Let him chop off a head just once. Then you do it, then me. (*Reluctantly, the Biggest Boy hands Michael the wooden sword and kneels down. The Fat Boy sits down, beats his thigh, and laughs with all his might. The Girl weeps loudly. Michael swings the big sword and "cuts off" the head. In doing so, he topples over.*)

THE BIGGEST BOY. Ow! I'll show you how to hit the *right* way! (*Michael runs away. The children run after him. Grusha laughs, following them with her eyes. On looking back, she sees Simon Shashava standing on the opposite bank. He wears a shabby uniform.*)

151

GRUSHA. Simon!

SIMON. Is that Grusha Vashnadze?

GRUSHA. Simon!

SIMON (*formally*). A good morning to the young lady. I hope she is well.

GRUSHA (*getting up gaily and bowing low*). A good morning to the soldier. God be thanked he has returned in good health.

SIMON. They found better fish, so they didn't eat me, said the haddock.

GRUSHA. Courage, said the kitchen boy. Good luck, said the hero.

SIMON. And how are things here? Was the winter bearable? The neighbor considerate?

GRUSHA. The winter was a trifle rough, the neighbor as usual, Simon.

SIMON. May one ask if a certain person is still in the habit of putting her leg in the water when rinsing the linen?

GRUSHA. The answer is no. Because of the eyes in the bushes.

SIMON. The young lady is speaking of soldiers. Here stands a paymaster.

GRUSHA. A job worth twenty piasters?

SIMON. And lodgings.

GRUSHA (*with tears in her eyes*). Behind the barracks under the date trees.

SIMON. Yes, there. I see that someone has kept her eyes open.

GRUSHA. Someone has.

SIMON. And has not forgotten? (*Grusha shakes her head.*) And so the door is still on its hinges as they say? (*Grusha looks at him in silence and shakes her head again.*) What's this? Is something not quite right?

GRUSHA. Simon Shashava, I can never return to Nuka. Something has happened.

SIMON. What has happened?

GRUSHA. For one thing, I knocked an Ironshirt down.

SIMON. Grusha Vashnadze must have had her reasons for that.

GRUSHA. Simon Shashava, I am no longer called what I used to be called.

SIMON (*after a pause*). I do not understand.

GRUSHA. When do women change their names, Simon? Let me explain it to you. Nothing stands between us. Everything has stayed just as it was. You've got to believe me.

SIMON. How can nothing stand between us and there still be something?

GRUSHA. How can I explain it to you so fast and with the stream between us? Couldn't you cross the bridge there?

SIMON. Perhaps it's no longer necessary.

GRUSHA. It is very necessary. Come over on this side, Simon. Quick!

SIMON. Does the young lady wish to say that someone has come too late?

(*Grusha looks up at him in despair, her face streaming with tears. Simon stares before him. He picks up a piece of wood and starts cutting it.*)

THE STORY TELLER.
So many words are said, so many left unsaid.
The soldier has come.
Where he comes from, he does not say.
Hear what he thought and did not say:
"The battle began gray at dawn, grew bloody at noon
The first fell before me, the second behind, the
    third at my side
On the first I stepped, the second I left, the
    third was run through by the captain
One brother of mine died by steel, the other by smoke
My neck was set aflame, my hands frozen in my gloves,
    my toes in my socks
I fed on aspen buds, I drank maple juice, I slept
    on stone, in water."

SIMON. I see a cap in the grass. Is there a little one already?

GRUSHA. There is, Simon. How could I hide it? But please don't worry, it is not mine.

SIMON. When the wind once begins to blow, they say, it blows through every cranny. The wife need say no more.

(*Grusha looks into her lap and is silent.*)

THE STORY TELLER.
There was yearning, but there was no waiting.
The oath is broken. No one could say why.
Hear what she thought but did not say:
"While you fought in the battle, soldier,
The bloody battle, the bitter battle
I found a child who was helpless
I had not the heart to destroy it.
I had to care for what had gone astray
I had to bend down for bread crumbs on the floor
I had to rend myself for that which was not mine
That which was strange.
Someone must be a helper.
For the little tree needs water
The lamb loses its way when the shepherd is asleep
And its cry is unheard!"

SIMON. Give me back the cross I gave you. Or, better, throw it into the stream. (*He turns to go.*)

GRUSHA (*getting up*). Simon Shashava, don't go away! It isn't mine! It isn't mine! (*She hears the children calling.*) What is the matter, children?

VOICES. Soldiers have come! They are taking Michael away!

(*Grusha stands aghast as two Ironshirts, with Michael between them, come toward her.*)

ONE OF THE IRONSHIRTS. Are you Grusha? (*She nods.*) Is this your child?

GRUSHA. Yes. (*Simon goes.*) Simon!

THE IRONSHIRT. We have orders, in the name of the law, to take this child, found in your charge, back to the city. It is suspected that the child is Michael Abashwili, son and heir of the late Governor Georgi Abashwili, and his wife, Natella Abashwili. Here is the document and the seal. (*They lead the child away.*)

GRUSHA (*running after them, shouting*). Leave it here. Please! It's mine!

THE STORY TELLER.
The Ironshirts took the child, the beloved child.

The unhappy girl followed them to the city,
   the dreaded city.
She who had borne him demanded the child.
She who had raised him faced trial.
Who will decide the case?
To whom will the child be assigned?
Who will the judge be? A good judge? A bad?
The city was in flames.
In the judge's seat sat Azdak.*

PART TWO

1

THE STORY OF THE JUDGE

THE STORY TELLER.
   Hear the story of the judge
   How he turned judge, how he passed judgment,
      what kind of judge he was.
   On that Easter Sunday of the great revolt, when the
      Grand Duke was overthrown
   And his Governor Abashwili, father of our child,
      lost his head
   The Village Recorder Azdak found in the woods a
      fugitive and hid him in his hut.

   (*Azdak, in rags and slightly drunk, is helping an old beggar
   into his cottage.*)

* The name *Azdak* should be accented on the second syllable.

AZDAK. Stop snorting, you're not a horse. And it won't do you any good with the police if you run like a snotty nose in April. Stand still, I say. (*He catches the Old Man, who has marched into the cottage as if he'd like to go through the walls.*) Sit down and feed. Here's a lump of cheese. (*From under some rags, in a chest, he fishes out some cheese, and the Old Man greedily begins to eat.*) Haven't eaten in a long time, huh? (*The Old Man growls.*) Why did you run like that, asshole? The cop wouldn't even have seen you.

THE OLD MAN. I had to.

AZDAK. Scared shitless? (*The Old Man stares, uncomprehending.*) Huh. Don't lick your chops like a Grand Duke. Or an old sow. I can't stand it. We have to take respectable stinkers as God made them, but not you! I once heard of a senior judge who farted at a public dinner just to show an independent spirit! Watching you eat like that gives me the most awful ideas. Why don't you say something? (*Sharply*) Show me your hand. Can't you hear? (*The Old Man slowly puts out his hand.*) White! So you're not a beggar at all! A fraud, a walking swindle! And I'm hiding you from the cops as though you were a honest man! Why have you been running like that if you're a landowner? For that's what you are. Don't deny it, I see it in your guilty face. (*He gets up.*) Get out! (*The Old Man looks at him uncertainly.*) What are you waiting for, peasant-flogger?

THE OLD MAN. Pursued. Need your undivided attention. Make proposition . . .

AZDAK. What do you want to make? A proposition? Well, if that isn't the height of insolence. He's making me a proposition! The bitten man scratches his fingers bloody, and the leech that's biting him makes a proposition! Get out, I tell you!

THE OLD MAN. Understand point of view. Persuasion! Pay a hundred thousand piasters for one night. Yes?

AZDAK. What, you think you can buy me? For a hundred thousand piasters? Let's say a hundred and fifty thousand. Where are they?

THE OLD MAN. Have not got them here. Of course. Will be sent. Hope do not doubt.

156

AZDAK. Doubt very much. Get out!
(*The Old Man gets up, waddles to the door. A voice is heard off stage.*)
A VOICE. Azdak!
(*The Old Man turns, waddles to the opposite corner, stands still.*)
AZDAK (*calling out*). I'm not in! (*He walks to door.*) So you're sniffing around here again, Shauwa?
POLICEMAN SHAUWA (*reproachfully*). You've caught another rabbit, Azdak. You promised me that it wouldn't happen again.
AZDAK (*severely*). Shauwa, don't talk about things you don't understand. The rabbit is a dangerous and destructive beast. It gorges itself on plants, especially on that species of plants known as — er — weeds. It must therefore be exterminated.
SHAUWA. Azdak, don't be so hard on me. I'll lose my job if I don't arrest you. I know you have a good heart.
AZDAK. I do *not* have a good heart! How often must I tell you I'm a man of intellect?
SHAUWA (*slyly*). I know, Azdak. You're a superior person. You say so yourself. I'm just a Christian and an ignoramus. And so I ask you: When a rabbit of the Prince's is stolen and I'm a policeman, what am I to do with the offending party?
AZDAK. Shauwa, Shauwa, shame on you. There you stand asking me a question! What could be more tempting? Suppose you were a women — let's say Nunowna, that bad girl — and you show me your thigh — Nunowna's thigh, that is — and ask me: What shall I do with my thigh, it itches? Is she as innocent as she pretends? No. I catch a rabbit, but you catch a man. Man is made in God's image. Not so a rabbit, you know that. I'm a rabbit-eater, but you're a man-eater, Shauwa. And God will pass judgment on you. Shauwa, go home and repent. No, stop, there's something . . . (*He looks at the Old Man who stands trembling in the corner.*) No, it's nothing. Go home and repent. (*He slams the door behind Shauwa.*) Now you're surprised, huh? Surprised I didn't hand you over? I couldn't bring myself to hand over a bed-bug to that beast! It goes against my grain. Don't tremble be-

157

cause of a cop. So old and still so scared? Finish your cheese, but eat it like a poor man, or else they'll still catch you. Must I even tell you how a poor man behaves? (*He pushes him down, and then gives him back the cheese.*) The box is the table. Lay your elbows on the table. Now encircle the cheese on the plate as if it might be snatched away from you at any moment — what right have *you* to be safe, huh? Now hold the knife like an undersized sickle, and give your cheese a troubled look because, like all beautiful things, it's already fading away. (*Azdak watches him.*) They're after you. That speaks in your favor. But how can we be sure they're not mistaken about you? In Tiflis one time they hanged a landowner, a Turk, who could prove he quartered his peasants instead of merely cutting them in half, as is the custom. And he squeezed twice the usual amount of taxes out of them. His zeal was above suspicion. And yet they hanged him like a common criminal — because he was a Turk — a thing he couldn't do much about. An injustice! He got onto the gallows by a sheer fluke. In short, I don't trust you.

THE STORY TELLER.

Thus Azdak gave the old beggar a bed,
And learned that old beggar was the old butcher, the
    Grand Duke himself,
And was ashamed.
He accused himself and ordered the policeman to take
    him to Nuka, to court, to be judged.

(*In the court of justice three Ironshirts sit drinking. From a beam hangs a man in judge's robes. Enter Azdak, in chains, dragging Shauwa behind him.*)

AZDAK (*shouting*). I have helped the Grand Duke, the Grand Thief, the Grand Butcher, to escape! In the name of justice I ask to be severely judged in public trial!

THE FIRST IRONSHIRT. Who's this queer bird?

SHAUWA. That's our Recorder, Azdak.

AZDAK. I am despicable! treacherous! branded! Tell them, flat-foot, how I insisted on being put in chains and brought to the capital. Because I sheltered the Grand Duke, the Grand Swindler by mistake. And how afterward I found out. Look,

158

a marked man is denouncing himself! Tell them how I forced you to walk with me half the night to clear the whole thing up.

SHAUWA. And all by threats. That wasn't nice of you, Azdak.

AZDAK. Shut your mouth, Shauwa. You don't understand. A new age has come. It'll go thundering over you. You're finished. The police will be wiped out — pouf! Everything will be gone into, everything brought into the open. A man will give himself up, and why? — because he couldn't escape the people in any case. (*To Shauwa*) Tell them how I have been shouting all along Shoemaker Street. (*With big gestures, looking at the Ironshirts*) "In ignorance I let the Grand Swindler escape! Tear me to pieces, brothers!" To get it in first.

THE FIRST IRONSHIRT. And what was their answer?

SHAUWA. They comforted him in Butcher Street, and they laughed themselves sick in Shoemaker Street. That's all.

AZDAK. But here with you it's different, I know you're like iron. Brothers, where's the judge? I must be tried.

THE FIRST IRONSHIRT (*pointing at the hanged man*). Here's the judge. And please stop "brothering" us. That's rather a sore spot this evening.

AZDAK. "Here's the judge." That's an answer never heard in Grusinia before. Townsman, where's His Excellency the Governor? (*Pointing to the floor*) Here's His Excellency, stranger. Where's the Chief Tax Collector? Where's the official Recruiting Officer? The Patriarch? The Chief of Police? Here, here, here — all here. Brothers, that's what I expected from you.

THE SECOND IRONSHIRT. Stop. What did you expect, funny man?

AZDAK. What happened in Persia, brother, what happened there.

THE SECOND IRONSHIRT. And what did happen in Persia?

AZDAK. Forty years ago. Everybody was hanged. Viziers, tax collectors. Everybody. My grandfather, a remarkable man by the way, saw it all. For three whole days. Everywhere.

THE SECOND IRONSHIRT. And who ruled when the Vizier was hanged?

AZDAK. A peasant.

159

THE SECOND IRONSHIRT. And who commanded the army?

AZDAK. A soldier, soldier.

THE SECOND IRONSHIRT. And who paid the wages?

AZDAK. A dyer. A dyer paid the wages.

THE SECOND IRONSHIRT. Wasn't it a weaver, maybe?

THE FIRST IRONSHIRT. And why did all this happen, Persian?

AZDAK. "Why did all this happen?" Must there be a special reason? Why do you scratch yourself, brother? War! Too long a war! And no justice! My grandfather brought back a song that tells how it was. I and my friend the policeman will sing it for you. (*To Shauwa*) And hold the rope tight. It's very suitable! (*He sings, with Shauwa holding the rope tight around him.*)

THE SONG OF INJUSTICE IN PERSIA

Why don't our sons bleed any more? Why don't our
daughters weep?
Why do only the slaughter-house calves have
blood in their veins?
Why do only the willows shed tears on Lake Urmi?
The king must have a new province, the peasant
must give up his savings.
That the roof of the world might be conquered, the
roof of the cottage is torn down.
Our men are carried to the ends of the earth, so that
great ones can eat at home.
The soldiers kill each other, the marshals salute
each other.
They bite the widow's tax money to see if it's good,
Their swords break.
The battle was lost, the helmets were paid for.
(*refrain*) Is it so? Is it so?

SHAUWA (*refrain*). Yes, yes, yes, yes, yes it's so.

AZDAK. Do you want to hear the rest of it?

(*The First Ironshirt nods.*)

THE SECOND IRONSHIRT (*to Shauwa*). Did he teach you that song?

160

SHAUWA. Yes, only my voice isn't very good.

THE SECOND IRONSHIRT. No. (*To Azdak*) Go on singing.

AZDAK. The second verse is about the peace. (*He sings.*)

The offices are packed, the officials overflow
into the streets.
The rivers jump their banks and ravage the fields.
Those who cannot let down their own trousers rule
countries.
They can't count up to four, but they devour
eight courses.
The corn farmers, looking round for buyers, see only
the starving.
The weavers go home from their looms in rags.
(*refrain*) Is it so? Is it so?

SHAUWA (*refrain*). Yes, yes, yes, yes, yes it's so.

AZDAK.

That's why our sons don't bleed any more, that's why
our daughters don't weep.
That's why only the slaughter-house calves have
blood in their veins,
And only the willows shed tears by Lake Urmi
toward morning.

THE FIRST IRONSHIRT. Are you going to sing that song here in
town?

AZDAK. Sure. What's wrong with it?

THE FIRST IRONSHIRT. Do you see how the sky's getting red?
(*Turning round, Azdak sees the sky red with fire.*) That's in
the suburbs. The carpet weavers have also caught the "Persian Sickness," and have asked if Prince Kazbeki isn't eating too many courses. And this morning they strung up the
city judge. We have beaten them to pulp for one hundred
piasters a man, you understand?

AZDAK (*after a pause*). I understand. (*He glances shyly round
and, creeping away, sits down in a corner, his head in his
hands.*)

THE IRONSHIRTS (*to each other*). If there ever was a trouble-
maker it's him.

— I'm sure he's come to the capital to fish in the troubled waters.

SHAUWA. I don't think he's a really bad character, gentlemen. Steals a few chickens here and there. And maybe a rabbit.

THE SECOND IRONSHIRT (*approaching Azdak*). You came to fish in the troubled waters, huh?

AZDAK (*looking up*). I don't know why I came.

THE SECOND IRONSHIRT. Are you maybe in with the carpet weavers?

(*Azdak shakes his head.*)

THE SECOND IRONSHIRT. And what about that song?

AZDAK. From my grandfather. A silly and ignorant man.

THE SECOND IRONSHIRT. Right. And what about the dyer who paid the wages?

AZDAK (*muttering*). That was in Persia.

THE FIRST IRONSHIRT. And what about your denouncing yourself? For not having hanged the Grand Duke with your own hands?

AZDAK. Didn't I tell you I let him run? (*He creeps farther away and sits on the floor.*)

SHAUWA. I swear to that. He let him run.

(*The Ironshirts burst out laughing and slap Shauwa on the back. Azdak laughs loudest. They slap Azdak too, and unchain him. They all start drinking as the Fat Prince enters with a young man.*)

THE FIRST IRONSHIRT (*to Azdak, pointing at the Fat Prince*). There you have your new age. (*More laughter.*)

THE FAT PRINCE. Well, my friends, what have you got to laugh about? Permit me a serious word. Yesterday morning the Princes of Grusinia overthrew the war-mongering government of the Grand Duke and did away with his Governors. Unfortunately the Grand Duke himself escaped. In this fateful hour our carpet weavers, those eternal trouble-makers, had the effrontery to stir up a rebellion and hang our universally loved city judge, our dear Illo Orbeliani. Ts — ts — ts. My friends, we need peace, peace, peace in Grusinia! And justice! Here I bring you my dear nephew, Bizergan Kazbeki. He's to be the new judge. A very gifted fellow. What do you say? I want your opinion. I say: Let the people decide.

THE SECOND IRONSHIRT. Does this mean we elect the judge?

THE FAT PRINCE. Precisely. The people propose a very gifted fellow. Confer among yourselves, my friends. (*The Ironshirts confer.*) Don't worry, foxy. The job's yours. And the moment we catch the Grand Duke we'll not have to kiss this rabble's ass any more.

THE IRONSHIRTS (*between themselves*). That'll be fun.

— They have their pants full because they haven't caught the Grand Duke.

— When the outlook isn't so bright, they say: "My friends!" and "Let the people decide!" Now he even wants justice for Grusinia! But fun is fun as long as it lasts! (*Pointing at Azdak*) He knows all about justice. Hey, rascal, would you like to have the nephew be judge?

AZDAK. Are you asking me? You're not asking me, huh?

THE IRONSHIRT. Why not? Anything for a joke!

AZDAK. I understand you want to test him to the marrow. Correct? Have you a criminal ready? An old hand? So the candidate can show what he knows?

THE SECOND IRONSHIRT. Let me see, we've a couple of doctors downstairs. Let's use them.

AZDAK. Stop! That's no good. You can't take real criminals till we're sure of the judge being appointed. He may be dumb, but he must be appointed or else the law is violated. The law is a very sensitive creature. Like the spleen, it must never be assaulted or — it's all over. You can hang those two. Why not? You won't have violated the law, because the judge wasn't there. Judgment must always be pronounced with absolute gravity — why? Because it's such nonsense. Suppose, for instance, a judge jails a woman that's stolen a corncake for her child, and the judge isn't wearing his robes. Maybe he's scratching himself while passing sentence and nearly half his body is uncovered — a man must scratch his thigh once in a while — then the sentence he passes is a disgrace

163

and the law is violated. It would be easier for a judge's robe and a judge's hat to pass judgment than for a mere man with no robe and no hat! If you don't watch out, the law just goes to pot. You don't try out a bottle of wine by offering it to a dog, and why not? Because you'd lose your wine.

THE FIRST IRONSHIRT. Then what do you suggest, hair-splitter?

AZDAK. I'll be the accused.

THE FIRST IRONSHIRT. You! (*He bursts out laughing.*)

THE FAT PRINCE. What have you decided?

THE FIRST IRONSHIRT. We've decided to have a tryout. Our friend will be the accused, and here's the judge's seat for the candidate.

THE FAT PRINCE. It isn't customary, but why not? (*To the Nephew*) A mere formality, foxy. What have you learned? Who got there first? The slow runner or the fast.

THE NEPHEW. The silent runner, Uncle Arsen.

(*The Nephew takes the chair. The Ironshirts and the Fat Prince sit on the steps. Enter Azdak, mimicking the gait of the Grand Duke.*)

AZDAK. Is there any here who knows me? I am the Grand Duke.

THE IRONSHIRTS. What is he?

— The Grand Duke. After all, he knows him.

— That's fine. Get on with the proceedings.

AZDAK. Listen! I'm accused of instigating a war. Ridiculous! Am saying "it's ridiculous!" That enough? If not, have brought lawyers in. Believe five hundred. (*He points behind him, pretending to be surrounded by lawyers.*) Requisition all available seats for lawyers!

(*The Ironshirts laugh; the Fat Prince joins in.*)

THE NEPHEW (*to the Ironshirts*). Do you want me to try this case? I must admit I find it rather unusual. From the taste angle, I mean.

THE FIRST IRONSHIRT. Let's go!

THE FAT PRINCE (*smiling*). Let him have it, foxy!

THE NEPHEW. All right. People of Grusinia versus Grand Prince. Defendant, what have you to say!

AZDAK. Plenty. Naturally, have read myself the war lost. Only

started it on the advice of patriots. Like Uncle Arsen Kazbeki. Demand Uncle Arsen as witness.

THE FAT PRINCE (*to the Ironshirts, delightedly*). What a screw-
ball!

THE NEPHEW. Motion rejected. You cannot be accused of de-
claring war, which every ruler has to do once in a while, but
only of conducting it badly.

AZDAK. Rubbish! Didn't conduct it at all! Had it conducted!
Had it conducted by Princes! Naturally they messed it up.

THE NEPHEW. Do you by any chance deny having been commander-in-chief?

AZDAK. Not at all! Always was commander-in-chief. At birth
shouted at wet nurse. Was trained to drop turds in toilet.
Grew accustomed to command. Always commanded officials
to rob my cash box. Officers flog soldiers only on command.
Landowners sleep with peasants' wives only on strictest command. Uncle Arsen here grew his belly only by my command!

THE IRONSHIRTS (*clapping*). He's good! Long live the Grand
Duke!

THE FAT PRINCE. Answer him, foxy! I'm with you.

THE NEPHEW. I shall answer him according to the dignity of
the law. Defendant, preserve the dignity of the law!

AZDAK. Agreed. I command you to proceed with the trial!

THE NEPHEW. It's not your place to command me. So you claim
that the Princes forced you to declare war. How can you
claim then that they — er —"messed it up"?

AZDAK. Didn't send enough people. Embezzled funds. Sent sick
horses. During attack, drinking in whore house. Propose Uncle Arsen as witness.

THE NEPHEW. Are you trying to make the outrageous claim
that the Princes of this country did not fight?

AZDAK. No. Princes fought. Fought for war contracts.

THE FAT PRINCE (*jumping up*). That's too much! This man
talks like a carpet weaver!

AZDAK. Really? Nothing but the truth!

THE FAT PRINCE. Hang him! Hang him!

THE FIRST IRONSHIRT (*pulling the Prince down*). Keep quiet! Go on, Excellency!

THE NEPHEW. Quiet! I now render a verdict: You must be hanged! By the neck! Having lost war!

AZDAK. Young man, seriously advise not to fall publicly into jerky and clipped manner of speech. Cannot be employed as watchdog if howl like wolf. Got it? If people realize Princes talk same language as Grand Duke, may hang Grand Duke *and* Princes, huh? By the way, must overrule verdict. Reason? War lost, but not for Princes. Princes have won *their* war. Got themselves paid 3,863,000 piasters for horses not delivered, 8,240,000 piasters for food supplies not produced. Are therefore victors. War lost only for Grusinia, which is not present in this court.

THE FAT PRINCE. I think that's enough, my friends. (*To Azdak*) You can withdraw, funny man. (*To the Ironshirts*) I think you cannot ratify the new judge's appointment, my friends.

THE FIRST IRONSHIRT. Yes, we can. Take down the judge's gown. (*One Ironshirt climbs on the back of the other, pulls the gown off the hanged man.*) And now (*To the Nephew*) you be off so the right ass can get on the right chair! (*To Azdak*) Step forward! Go to the judge's seat and sit up there, man. (*Azdak steps up, bows, and sits down.*) The judge was always a rascal! Now the rascal shall be a judge! (*The judge's gown is placed round his shoulders, the hat on his head.*) And what a judge!

THE STORY TELLER.
    And there was civil war in the land.
    The ruler was unsafe.
    And Azdak was made a judge by the Ironshirts.
    And Azdak remained a judge for two years.

THE STORY TELLER AND CHORUS.
    Conflagration's heat, and blood in every street,
        And cockroach and bug in every town.
    In the castle, fànatics. At the altar, heretics.
    And Azdak wearing a judge's gown.

(*Azdak sits in the judge's chair, peeling an apple. Shauwa*

166

is sweeping out the hall. On one side an invalid in a wheel-chair. Opposite, a young man accused of blackmail. An Iron-shirt stands on guard, holding the Ironshirt's banner.)

AZDAK. In consideration of the large number of cases, the Court today will hear two cases at a time. Before I open the proceedings, a short announcement — I accept — (*He stretches out his hand. The Blackmailer is the only one to produce any money. He hands it to Azdak.*) — I reserve for myself the right to punish one of the parties here for contempt of court. (*He glances at the Invalid.*) You (*To the Doctor*) are a doctor, and you (*To the Invalid*) are bringing a complaint against him. Is the doctor responsible for your condition?

THE INVALID. Yes. I had a stroke because of him.

AZDAK. That would be professional negligence.

THE INVALID. More than negligence. I gave this man money for his studies. So far, he hasn't paid me back a cent. And when I heard he was treating a patient free, I had a stroke.

AZDAK. Rightly. (*To a limping man*) And you, what do you want here?

THE LIMPING MAN. I'm the patient, your honor.

AZDAK. He treated your leg for nothing?

THE LIMPING MAN. The wrong leg! My rheumatism was in the left leg, and he operated on the right. That's why I limp now.

AZDAK. And you got it free?

THE INVALID. A five-hundred-piaster operation free! For nothing! For a God-bless-you! And I paid for this man's studies! (*To the Doctor*) Did they teach you to operate free?

THE DOCTOR. Your Honor, it is actually the custom to demand the fee before the operation, as the patient is more willing to pay before an operation than after. Which is only human. In the case in question I was convinced, when I started the operation, that my servant had already received the fee. In this I was mistaken.

THE INVALID. He was mistaken! A good doctor doesn't make mistakes! He examines before he operates.

AZDAK. That's right. (*To Shauwa*) Public Prosecutor, what's the other case about?

167

SHAUWA (*busily sweeping*). Blackmail.

THE BLACKMAILER. High Court of Justice, I'm innocent. I only wanted to find out from the landowner concerned if he really had raped his niece. He informed me very politely that this was not the case, and gave me the money only so I could pay for my uncle's studies.

AZDAK. Hm. (*To the Doctor*) You, on the other hand, can cite no extenuating circumstances for your offense, huh?

THE DOCTOR. Except that to err is human.

AZDAK. And you are perfectly well aware that in money matters a good doctor is conscious of his responsibility? I once heard of a doctor who made a thousand piasters out of one sprained finger: he discovered it had something to do with blood circulation, which a less good doctor might have overlooked. On another occasion he made a real gold mine out of the careful treatment of a somewhat disordered gall bladder. You have no excuse, Doctor. The corn merchant, Uxu, had his son study medicine to get some knowledge of trade, our medical schools are so good. (*To the Blackmailer*) What's the name of the landowner?

SHAUWA. He doesn't want it known.

AZDAK. In that case I will pass judgment. The Court considers the blackmail proved. And you (*to the Invalid*) are sentenced to a fine of one thousand piasters. If you get a second stroke, the doctor will have to treat you free. Eventually he will have to amputate. (*To the Limping Man*) As compensation, you will receive a bottle of rubbing alcohol. (*To the Blackmailer*) You are sentenced to hand over half the proceeds of your deal to the Public Prosecutor to keep the landowner's name secret. You are advised, moreover, to study medicine — you seem well suited to that calling. (*To the Doctor*) You are acquitted in consideration of an unpardonable error in the practice of your profession! Next cases!

THE STORY TELLER AND CHORUS.

With a pound you're on firm ground (no one is willing
for a shilling)
And the law is a cat in a sack.

168

But one whelp brings help to the many for a penny.
The name of this rascal? Azdak.

(*Enter Azdak from the caravansary on the highroad, followed by an old bearded innkeeper. The judge's chair is carried
by a stableman and Shauwa. An Ironshirt, with a banner,
takes up his position.*)

AZDAK. Put it here. Then we'll get some air and maybe a good
breeze from the lemon grove over there. It does justice good
to be administered in the open: the wind blows her skirts up
and you can see what she's got underneath. Shauwa, we've
eaten too much. These official journeys are very exhausting.
(*To the Innkeeper*) Where's your daughter-in-law?

THE INNKEEPER. Your Worship, it's a question of the family
honor. I wish to bring an action on behalf of my son, who's
on business on the other side of the mountain. This is the
offending stableman, and here's my daughter-in-law.

(*Enter the Daughter-in-law, a voluptuous wench. She is
veiled.*)

AZDAK (*sitting down*). I accept . . . (*Sighing, the Innkeeper
hands him some money.*) Good. Now the formalities are dis-
posed of. This is a case of rape?

THE INNKEEPER. Your Honor, I caught the fellow in the act.
Ludovica was already in the straw on the stable floor.

AZDAK. Quite right, the stable. Beautiful horses! I particularly
liked the little roan.

THE INNKEEPER. The first thing I did, of course, was question
Ludovica. On my son's behalf.

AZDAK (*seriously*). I said I particularly liked it.

THE INNKEEPER (*coldly*). Really? Ludovica confessed the stableman took her against her will.

AZDAK. Take your veil off, Ludovica. (*She does so.*) Ludovica,
you please the Court. Tell us how it happened.

LUDOVICA (*well-schooled*). When I entered the stable to see the
new foal the stableman said to me on his own accord: "It's
hot today!" and laid his hand on my left breast. I said to
him: "Don't do that!" But he continued to handle me inde-
cently, which provoked my anger. Before I realized his sin-

ful intentions, he had got much closer. It had already taken place when my father-in-law entered and accidentally trod on me.

THE INNKEEPER (*explaining*). On my son's behalf.

AZDAK (*to the Stableman*). Do you admit you started it?

THE STABLEMAN. Yes.

AZDAK. Ludovica, do you like to eat sweet things?

LUDOVICA. Yes, sunflower seeds!

AZDAK. Do you like to lie a long time in the bathtub?

LUDOVICA. Half an hour or so.

AZDAK. Public Prosecutor, drop your knife — there — on the floor. (*Shauwa does so.*) Ludovica, go and pick up the knife. (*Ludovica, swaying her hips, does so.*) See that? (*He points at her.*) The way it moves? The rape is now proven. By eating too much — sweet things, especially — by lying too long in warm water, by laziness and too soft a skin, you have raped that unfortunate man. Do you imagine you can run around with a behind like that and get away with it in court? This is a case of intentional assault with a dangerous weapon! You are sentenced to hand over to the Court the little roan which your father liked to ride "on his son's behalf." And now, come with me to the stables, so the Court may inspect the scene of the crime, Ludovica.

THE STORY TELLER AND CHORUS.

When visiting your neighbor sharpen up your ax,
For Bible texts and sermons are trivial knickknacks.
What miracles past believing the ax's edge can do!
Sometimes Azdak believed in miracles too.

(*Azdak's judge's chair is in a tavern. Three rich farmers stand before Azdak. Shauwa brings him wine. In a corner stands an old peasant woman. In the open doorway, and outside, stand villagers looking on. An Ironshirt stands guard with a banner.*)

AZDAK. The Public Prosecutor has the floor.

SHAUWA. It concerns a cow. For five weeks the defendant has had a cow in her stable, the property of the farmer Suru. She was also found to be in possession of a stolen ham, and a

170

number of cows belonging to Shutoff were killed after he
had asked the defendant to pay the rent on a piece of land.

THE FARMERS. It's a matter of my ham, Your Honor.

— It's a matter of my cow, Your Honor.

— It's a matter of my land, Your Honor.

AZDAK. Well, Granny, what have you got to say to all this?

THE OLD WOMAN. Your Honor, one night toward morning, five
weeks ago, there was a knock at my door, and outside stood
a bearded man with a cow, and said: "My dear woman, I
am the miracle-working Saint Banditus and because your son
has been killed in the war, I bring you this cow as a souvenir.
Take good care of it."

THE FARMERS. The robber, Irakli, Your Honor!

— Her brother-in-law, Your Honor!

— The cow-thief!

— The incendiary!

— He must be beheaded!

(*Outside, a woman screams. The crowd grows restless, retreats. Enter the bandit Irakli with a huge ax.*)

THE BANDIT. A very good evening, dear friends! A glass of
vodka!

THE FARMERS (*crossing themselves*). Irakli!

AZDAK. Public Prosecutor, a glass of vodka for our guest. And
who are you?

THE BANDIT. I'm a wandering hermit, Your Honor. And thank
you for the gracious gift. (*He empties the glass which Shauwa has brought.*) Another!

AZDAK. I am Azdak. (*He gets up and bows. The Bandit also
bows.*) The Court welcomes the foreign hermit. Go on with
your story, Granny.

THE OLD WOMAN. Your Honor, that first night I didn't yet know
that Saint Banditus could work miracles, it was only the cow.
But one night, a few days later, the farmer's servants came
to take the cow away again. Then they turned round in front
of my door and went off without the cow. And on their heads
sprouted bumps big as a fist. Then I knew that Saint Banditus had changed their hearts and turned them into friendly
people.

171

(*The Bandit roars with laughter.*)

THE FIRST FARMER. I know what changed them.

AZDAK. That's fine. You can tell us later. Continue.

THE OLD WOMAN. Your Honor, the next one to become a good man was the farmer Shutoff — a devil, as everyone knows. But Saint Banditus has arranged it so that he let me off the rent on the little piece of land.

THE SECOND FARMER. Because my cows were killed in the field. (*The Bandit laughs.*)

THE OLD WOMAN (*answering Azdak's sign to continue*). And then one morning the ham came flying in at my window. It hit me in the small of the back. I'm still lame from it, see, Your Honor. (*She limps a few steps. The Bandit laughs.*) I ask Your Honor, was there ever a time when a poor old woman could get a ham without a miracle? (*The Bandit starts sobbing.*)

AZDAK (*rising from his chair*). Granny, that's a question that strikes straight at the Court's heart. Be so kind as to sit down here. (*Hesitating, the Old Woman sits in the judge's chair. Azdak sits on the floor, glass in hand, reciting.*)

> Granny, I almost called you Mother Grusinia
> the Woebegone,
> The bereaved one, whose sons are at the war.
> She is beaten with fists, but full of hope!
> She weeps when she receives a cow
> And is surprised when she is not beaten.
> When you judge us be merciful, Granny!

(*Bellowing at the Farmers*) Admit that you don't believe in miracles, you atheists! Each of you is sentenced to pay five hundred piasters! For your godlessness! Get out! (*The Farmers slink out.*) And you Granny, and you (*to the Bandit*) pious man, empty a pitcher of wine with the Public Prosecutor and Azdak!

THE STORY TELLER AND CHORUS.

> Statute and rule he broke like a loaf to feed the folk.
> On the wreck of the law he brought them to the shore,

Granted their shrill demands, took bribes from the
  empty hands
Of the simple and the poor.

Two years and more Azdak was a wolf to the wolf pack
And weighed with a false scale.
In the judge's seat he'd stay — the gallows not
  far away —
The law had a sting in its tail.

THE STORY TELLER.
  But the era of disorder came to an end.
  The Grand Duke returned,
  The Governor's wife returned.
  A Trial was held.
  Many people died.
  The suburbs burned anew.
  And fear seized Azdak.

(*Azdak's judge's chair stands again in the court of justice.
Azdak sits on the floor, shaving and talking to Shauwa.
Noises outside. In the rear the Fat Prince's head is carried
by on a lance.*)

AZDAK. Shauwa, the days of your slavery are numbered, maybe
even the minutes. For a long time I have held you in the iron
curb of reason, and it has torn your mouth till it bleeds. I
have lashed you with reasonable arguments and manhandled
you with logic. You are by nature a weak man, and if one
slyly throws an argument in your path, you have to snap it
up. You can't resist. By nature, you have to lick the hand of
a superior being, but superior beings can be of very different
kinds. And now with your liberation, you will soon be able to
follow your inclinations, which are low. You will be able to
follow your infallible instinct, which teaches you to plant
your fat heel on the faces of men. Gone is the era of confusion and disorder, which I find described in the Song of
Chaos. Let us now sing that song together in memory of those
terrible days. Sit down and don't do violence to the music.
Don't be afraid. It sounds all right. And it has a fine refrain.
(*He sings.*)

173

Sister, hide your face! Brother, take your knife!
The times are out of joint!
Big men are full of complaints
And small men full of joy.
The city says:
"Let us drive the strong ones from our midst!"
Offices are raided. Lists of serfs are destroyed.
They have set Master's nose to the grindstone.
They who lived in the dark have seen the light.
The ebony poor box is broken.
Sesnem wood is sawed up for beds.
Who had no bread have barns full.
Who begged for alms of corn now mete it out.

SHAUWA (*refrain*). Oh, oh, oh, oh.

AZDAK (*refrain*).
Where are you, General, where are you?
Please, please, please, restore order!

The nobleman's son can no longer be recognized;
The lady's child becomes the son of her slave.
The councilors meet in a shed.
Once, this man was barely allowed to sleep on the wall;
Now, he stretches his limbs in a bed.
Once, this man rowed a boat; now, he owns ships.
Their owner looks for them, but they're his no longer.
Five men are sent on a journey by their master.
"Go yourself," they say, "We have arrived."

SHAUWA (*refrain*). Oh, oh, oh, oh.

AZDAK (*refrain*).
Where are you, General, where are you?
Please, please, please, restore order!

Yes. So it might have been, had order been neglected much
longer. But now the Grand Duke has returned to the capital,
and the Persians have lent him an army to restore order with.
The suburbs are already aflame. Go and get me the big book
I always sit on. (*Shauwa brings the big book from the*

174

judge's chair. Azdak opens it.) This is the Statute Book and I've always used it, as you can bear witness. Now I'd better look and see what they can do to me. I've let the down-and-outs get away with murder, and I'll have to pay for it. I helped poverty onto its skinny legs, so they'll hang me for drunkenness. I peeped into the rich man's pocket, which is bad taste. And I can't hide anywhere — everybody knows me because I have helped everybody.

SHAUWA. Someone's coming!

AZDAK (*in panic, he walks trembling to the chair*). The end! And now they'd enjoy seeing what a Great Man I am. I'll deprive them of that pleasure. I'll beg on my knees for mercy. Spittle will slobber down my chin. The fear of death is in me. (*Enter Natella Abashwili, the Governor's Wife, followed by the Adjutant and an Ironshirt.*)

THE GOVERNOR'S WIFE. What sort of a creature is that, Shalva?

AZDAK. A willing one, Your Highness, a man ready to oblige.

THE ADJUTANT. Natella Abashwili, wife of the late Governor, has just returned and is looking for her two-year-old son, Michael. She has been informed that the child was carried off to the mountains by a former servant.

AZDAK. It will be brought back, Your Highness, at your service.

THE ADJUTANT. They say that the person in question is passing it off as her own child.

AZDAK. She will be beheaded, Your Highness, at your service.

THE ADJUTANT. That is all.

THE GOVERNOR'S WIFE (*leaving*). I don't like that man.

AZDAK (*following her to door, bowing*). At your service, Your Highness, it will all be arranged.

THE CHALK CIRCLE

THE STORY TELLER.

> Hear now the story of the trial
> Concerning Governor Abashwili's child
> And the establishing of the true mother
> By the famous test of the Chalk Circle.

(*The court of justice in Nuka. Ironshirts lead Michael across stage and out at the back. Ironshirts hold Grusha back with their lances under the gateway until the child has been led through. Then she is admitted. She is accompanied by the former Governor's cook. Distant noises and a fire-red sky.*)

GRUSHA (*trying to hide*). He's brave, he can wash himself already.

THE COOK. You're lucky. It's not a real judge. It's Azdak. Just a drunk who doesn't understand a thing. The biggest thieves have got by through him. Because he mixes everything up and the rich never offer him big enough bribes, the likes of us sometimes get off pretty well.

GRUSHA. Today I *need* luck.

THE COOK. Touch wood. (*She crosses herself.*) I'd better offer up another prayer that the judge may be drunk. (*She prays with motionless lips, while Grusha looks around, in vain, for the child.*)

THE COOK. What I can't understand is why you must hold on to it at any price if it isn't yours. In days like these.

GRUSHA. He's mine. I brought him up.

THE COOK. But have you never thought what'd happen when she came back?

GRUSHA. At first I thought I'd give him back to her. Then I thought she *wouldn't* come back.

THE COOK. And even a borrowed coat keeps a man warm, hm? (*Grusha nods.*) I'll swear to anything for you. You're a decent girl. (*She sees the soldier Simon Shashava approach-*

176

ing.) You have done a great wrong by Simon. I've talked with him. He can't understand it.

GRUSHA (*unaware of Simon's presence*). Just now I can't be bothered with him if he can't understand.

THE COOK. He has understood the child is not yours, but you married and not free until death you do part — he can't understand that.

(*Grusha sees Simon and greets him.*)

SIMON (*gloomily*). I wanted to inform the lady I am ready to swear I am the father of the child.

GRUSHA (*low*). That's right, Simon.

SIMON. At the same time I would like to inform the lady that I am not hereby bound to anything — nor she either.

THE COOK. That's unnecessary. She's married. You know that.

SIMON. That's her business and needs no rubbing in.

(*Enter an Ironshirt.*)

THE IRONSHIRT. Where's the judge? Has anyone seen the judge?

ANOTHER IRONSHIRT (*stepping forward*). The judge isn't here. There's nothing but a bed and a pitcher in the whole house.

(*Exeunt Ironshirts.*)

THE COOK. I hope nothing has happened to him. With any other judge you'd have about as much chance as a chicken has teeth.

GRUSHA (*who has turned away and covered her face*). Stand in front of me. I shouldn't have come to Nuka. If I run into the Ironshirt, the one I hit over the head . . .

(*She screams. An Ironshirt had stopped and, turning his back, had been listening to her. He now wheels around. It is the Corporal, and he has a huge scar across his face.*)

THE IRONSHIRT (*in the gateway*). What's the matter, Shotta? Do you know her?

THE CORPORAL (*after staring for some time*). No.

THE IRONSHIRT. She's the one who's supposed to have stolen the Abashwili child. If you know anything about it you can make a heap of money, Shotta. (*Exit the Corporal, cursing.*)

THE COOK. Was it him? (*Grusha nods.*) I think he'll keep his mouth shut, or he'd be admitting he was after the child.

177

GRUSHA. I'd almost forgotten already that I saved the child from them.

(*Enter the Governor's Wife, followed by the Adjutant and two lawyers.*)

THE GOVERNOR'S WIFE. At least there are no *common* people here, thank God. I can't stand their smell. It always gives me migraine.

THE FIRST LAWYER. Madam, I must ask you to be as careful as possible in everything you say until we have another judge.

THE GOVERNOR'S WIFE. But I didn't say anything at all, Illo Shuboladze. I *love* the people with their simple straightforward minds! It's only that their smell brings on my migraine.

THE SECOND LAWYER. There won't be many spectators. The population is sitting at home behind locked doors because of the riots in the suburbs.

THE GOVERNOR'S WIFE (*looking at Grusha*). Is that the creature?

THE FIRST LAWYER. Please, most gracious Natella Abashwili, I must ask you to abstain from all invective, until it is absolutely certain that the Grand Duke has appointed a new judge, and we've got rid of the present one who is about the lowest ever seen in a judge's gown. And things seem all set to move, you see.

(*Enter Ironshirts from the courtyard.*)

THE COOK. Her Grace would pull your hair out on the spot if she didn't know Azdak is for the poor people. He goes by the face.

(*Ironshirts begin fastening a rope to a beam. Azdak, in chains, is led in, followed by Shauwa, also in chains. The three farmers bring up the rear.*)

AN IRONSHIRT. You were trying to run away, it seems. (*He strikes Azdak.*)

ONE FARMER. Off with the judge's gown before we string him up. (*Ironshirts and farmers tear off Azdak's gown. His torn underwear is visible. Then someone kicks him.*)

AN IRONSHIRT (*pushing him into someone else*). If you want a heap of justice, here it is!

(*Accompanied by shouts of* "You'll get it!" *and* "Let me have him, brother!" *they throw Azdak back and forth until he collapses. Then he is lifted up and dragged under the noose.*)

THE GOVERNOR'S WIFE (*who, during this "ball-game," has clapped her hands hysterically*). I disliked that man from the moment I first saw him.

AZDAK (*covered with blood, panting*). I can't see. Give me a rag.

AN IRONSHIRT. What is it you want to see?

AZDAK. You dogs! (*He wipes the blood out of his eyes with his shirt.*) Good morning, dogs! How goes it, dogs! How's the dog world? Does it smell good? Have you another boot to lick? Are you back at each other's throats, dogs?

(*Accompanied by a corporal, a dust-covered rider enters. He takes some documents from a leather case, looks at them, then interrupts.*)

THE RIDER. Stop! I bring a dispatch from the Grand Duke, containing the latest appointments.

THE CORPORAL (*bellowing*). Atten — shun!

THE RIDER. Of the new judge it says: "We appoint a man whom we have to thank for the saving of a life indispensable to the country's welfare — a certain Azdak of Nuka." Which is he?

SHAUWA (*pointing*). That's him, Your Excellency.

THE CORPORAL (*bellowing*). What's going on here?

AN IRONSHIRT. I ask to be allowed to report that His Honor Azdak was already His Honor Azdak, but on these farmers' denunciation was pronounced the Grand Duke's enemy.

THE CORPORAL (*pointing at the farmers*). March them off! (*They are marched off. They bow all the time.*) See to it that His Honor Azdak is exposed to no more violence. (*Exeunt Rider and Corporal.*)

THE COOK (*to Shauwa*). She clapped her hands! I hope he saw it!

THE FIRST LAWYER. It's a catastrophe.

(*Azdak has fainted. Coming to, he is dressed again in judge's robes. He walks, swaying, toward the Ironshirts.*)

179

AN IRONSHIRT. What does Your Honor desire?

AZDAK. Nothing, fellow dogs. An occasional boot to lick. (*To Shauwa*) I pardon you. (*He is unchained.*) Get me some red wine, the sweet kind. (*Shauwa stumbles off.*) Get out of here, I've got to judge a case. (*Exeunt Ironshirts. Shauwa returns with a pitcher of wine. Azdak gulps it down.*) Something for my backside!

(*Shauwa brings the statute book, puts it on the judge's chair. Azdak sits on it.*) I accept . . .

(*The prosecutors, among whom a worried council has been held, smile with relief. They whisper.*)

THE COOK. Oh dear!

SIMON. A well can't be filled with dew! they say.

THE LAWYERS (*approaching Azdak, who stands up, expectantly*). A quite ridiculous case, Your Honor. The accused has abducted a child and refuses to hand it over.

AZDAK (*stretching out his hand, glancing at Grusha*). A most attractive person. (*He fingers the money, then sits down, satisfied.*) I open the proceedings and demand the absolute truth. (*To Grusha*) Especially from you.

THE FIRST LAWYER. High Court of Justice! Blood, as the popular saying goes, is thicker than water. This old adage . . .

AZDAK (*interrupting*). The Court wants to know the lawyers' fee.

THE FIRST LAWYER (*surprised*). I beg your pardon? (*Azdak, smiling, rubs his thumb and index finger.*) Oh, I see. Five hundred piasters, Your Honor, to answer the Court's somewhat unusual question.

AZDAK. Did you hear? The question is unusual. I ask it because I listen to you in quite a different way when I know you are good.

THE FIRST LAWYER (*bowing*). Thank you, Your Honor. High Court of Justice, of all ties the ties of blood are strongest. Mother and child — is there a more intimate relationship? Can one tear a child from its mother? High Court of Justice, she has conceived it in the holy ecstasies of love. She has carried it in her womb. She has fed it with her blood. She has

180

borne it with pain. High Court of Justice, it has been observed that even the wild tigress, robbed of her young, roams restless through the mountains, shrunk to a shadow. Nature herself . . .

AZDAK (*interrupting, to Grusha*). What's your answer to all this and anything else the lawyer might have to say?

GRUSHA. He's mine.

AZDAK. Is that all? I hope you can prove it. In any case, I advise you to tell me why you think I should assign the child to you.

GRUSHA. I brought him up like the priest says "according to my best knowledge and conscience." I always found him something to eat. Most of the time he had a roof over his head. And I went to such trouble for him. I had expenses too. I didn't look out for my own comfort. I brought the child up to be friendly with everyone, and from the beginning taught him to work as well as he could. He's still a very little thing.

THE FIRST LAWYER. Your Honor, it is significant that the girl herself doesn't claim any tie of blood between her and the child.

AZDAK. The Court takes note.

THE FIRST LAWYER. Thank you, Your Honor. Please permit a woman bowed in sorrow — who has already lost her husband and now has also to fear the loss of her child — to address a few words to you. The gracious Natella Abashwili is . . .

THE GOVERNOR'S WIFE (*quietly*). A most cruel fate, Sir, forces me to ask you to return my beloved child. It is not for me to describe to you the tortures of a bereaved mother's soul, the anxiety, the sleepless nights, the . . .

THE SECOND LAWYER (*bursting out*). It's outrageous the way this woman is being treated. She is not allowed to enter her husband's palace. The revenue of her estates is blocked. She is cold-bloodedly told that it's tied to the heirs. She can't do anything without the child. She can't even pay her lawyers! (*To the First Lawyer who, desperate about this outburst, makes frantic gestures to keep him from speaking*) Dear Illo

Shuboladze, why shouldn't it be divulged now that it's the Abashwili estates that are at stake?

THE FIRST LAWYER. Please, Honored Sandro Oboladze! We had agreed . . . (*To Azdak*) Of course it is correct that the trial will also decide whether our noble client will obtain the right to dispose of the extensive Abashwili estates. I say "also" advisedly, for in the foreground stands the human tragedy of a mother, as Natella Abashwili rightly explained in the first words of her moving statement. Even if Michael Abashwili were *not* the heir of the estates, he would still be the dearly beloved child of my client.

AZDAK. Stop! The Court is touched by the mention of the estates. It's a proof of human feeling.

THE SECOND LAWYER. Thanks, Your Honor. Dear Illo Shuboladze, we can prove in any case that the woman who took possession of the child is not the child's mother. Permit me to lay before the Court the bare facts. High Court of Justice, by an unfortunate chain of circumstances, the child Michael Abashwili was left behind while its mother was making her escape. Grusha, a palace kitchen maid, was present on that Easter Sunday and was observed to be busy with the child and . . .

THE COOK. All her mistress was thinking about was what kind of dresses she'd take along!

THE SECOND LAWYER (*unmoved*). Nearly a year later Grusha turned up in a mountain village with a child, and there entered into the state of matrimony with . . .

AZDAK. How did you get into that mountain village?

GRUSHA. On foot, Your Honor. And he was mine.

SIMON. I am the father, Your Honor.

THE COOK. He was in my care, Your Honor, for five piasters.

THE SECOND LAWYER. This man is engaged to Grusha, High Court of Justice, and therefore his testimony is not trustworthy.

AZDAK. Are you the man she married in the mountain village?

SIMON. No, Your Honor, she married a peasant.

AZDAK (*to Grusha*). Why? (*Pointing at Simon*) Is he no good in bed? Tell the truth.

182

GRUSHA. We didn't get that far. I married because of the child. So he should have a roof over his head. (*Pointing at Simon*) He was in the war, Your Honor.

AZDAK. And now he wants you again, huh?

SIMON. I wish to state in evidence . . .

GRUSHA (*angrily*). I am no longer free, Your Honor.

AZDAK. And the child, you claim, comes from whoring? (*Grusha doesn't answer.*) I'm going to ask you a question: What kind of a child is it? Is it a ragged little bastard or a child from a well-to-do family?

GRUSHA (*angrily*). He's just an ordinary child.

AZDAK. I mean — did he have refined features from the beginning?

GRUSHA. He had a nose on his face.

AZDAK. I consider that answer of yours important. It was said of me that once, before rendering a verdict, I went out and sniffed at a rosebush — tricks like that are necessary nowadays. Well, I'll make it short now, and not listen to any more lies. (*To Grusha*) Especially not yours. (*To all the accused*) I can imagine what you've cooked up to cheat me! I know you! You're swindlers.

GRUSHA (*suddenly*). I can quite understand your wanting to cut it short, now I've seen what you accepted!

AZDAK. Shut up! Did I accept anything from you?

GRUSHA (*while the Cook tries to restrain her*). I haven't got anything.

AZDAK. That's true. Quite true. From starvelings I never get a thing. I might just as well starve, myself. You want justice, but do you want to pay for it? When you go to the butcher you know you have to pay, but you go to the judge as if you were going to a funeral supper.

SIMON (*loudly*). When the horse was shod, the horse-fly held out its leg, as the saying is.

AZDAK (*eagerly accepting the challenge*). Better a treasure in manure than a stone in a mountain stream.

SIMON. A fine day. Let's go fishing, said the angler to the worm.

AZDAK. I'm my own master, said the servant, and cut off his foot.

SIMON. I love you as a father, said the Czar to the peasants, and had the Czarevitch's head chopped off.

AZDAK. A fool's worst enemy is himself.

SIMON. However, a fart has no nose.

AZDAK. Fined ten piasters for indecent language in Court! That'll teach you what justice is.

GRUSHA (*furiously*). A fine kind of justice! You play fast and loose with us because we don't talk as refined as that crowd with their lawyers!

AZDAK. That's so. You people are too dumb. It's only right you should get it in the neck.

GRUSHA. Because you want to pass the child on to her. And she's too refined to know how to keep it dry! You know no more about justice than I do, I can see.

AZDAK. There's something in that. I'm an ignorant man. I haven't even a decent pair of pants under my gown. See for yourself! With me, everything goes for food and drink — I was educated at a convent. Incidentally, I'll fine you ten piasters for contempt of court. And moreover you're a very silly girl, to turn me against you, instead of making eyes at me and wiggling your backside a little to keep me in a good temper. Twenty piasters!

GRUSHA. Even if it were thirty, I would tell you what I think of your justice, you drunken onion! (*Incoherently*) How dare you talk to me like the cracked Isaiah on the church window? As if you *were* somebody? When they pulled you out of your mother, it wasn't planned you should be rude and smack her on the fingers if she picked up a bowl of salt some place! Aren't you ashamed of yourself when you see how I tremble before you? You have made yourself their servant so no one should take their houses away, and they'd stolen them! Since when have houses belonged to bedbugs? But you're on the watch, or they couldn't drag our men into their wars! You bribe-taker! (*Azdak half gets up, starts beaming. With his little hammer he half-heartedly knocks on the table as if to get silence. As Grusha's scolding continues, he only beats time with his hammer.*) I've no respect for you. No more than for a thief or a robber with a knife! You can do what

184

you want. You can take the child away from me, a hundred against one, but I tell you one thing: only extortioners should be chosen for a profession like yours, and men who rape children! As punishment! They should sit in judgment on their fellow creatures. Which is worse than to hang from gallows.

AZDAK (*sitting down*). Now it'll be thirty! And I won't go on squabbling with you as though we were in a saloon. What'd happen to my dignity as a judge? Anyway, I've lost interest in your case. Where's the couple who wanted a divorce? (*To Shauwa*) Bring 'em in. This case is adjourned for fifteen minutes.

THE FIRST LAWYER (*to the Governor's Wife*). Even without using the rest of the evidence, Madam, we have the verdict in the bag.

THE COOK (*to Grusha*). You've gone and spoiled your chances with him. You won't get the child now.

THE GOVERNOR'S WIFE. Shalva, my smelling salts!

(*Enter a very old couple.*)

AZDAK. I accept . . . (*The Old Couple don't understand.*) I hear you want to be divorced. How long have you been living together?

THE OLD WOMAN. Forty years, Your Honor.

AZDAK. And why do you want a divorce?

THE OLD MAN. We don't like each other, Your Honor.

AZDAK. Since when?

THE OLD WOMAN. Oh, from the very beginning, Your Honor.

AZDAK. I'll think about your request and render my verdict when I'm through with the other case. (*Shauwa leads them back.*) I need the child. (*He beckons Grusha to him, and bends not unkindly toward her.*) I've noticed you have a soft spot for justice. I don't believe he's your child, but if he were yours, woman, wouldn't you want him to be rich? You'd only have to say he isn't yours. And immediately he'd have a palace and many horses in his stable and many beggars on his doorstep and many soldiers in his service and many petitioners in his courtyard, wouldn't he? What do you say — don't you want him to be rich?

185

(*Grusha is silent.*)

THE STORY TELLER. Hear now what the angry girl thought but did not say:

> "If he went in golden shoes
> He would cruel be
> Evil then would be his life.
> He could laugh at me.

> "Too heavy is a heart of stone
> For human breast to bear!
> Bad and powerful to be
> Is too great a care.

> "Hunger he will have to fear
> But no hungry one!
> Darkness he will have to fear
> But not the sun!"

AZDAK. I think I understand you, woman.

GRUSHA (*suddenly and loudly*). I won't give him up. I've raised him, and he knows me.

(*Enter Shauwa with the child.*)

THE GOVERNOR'S WIFE. It's in rags!

GRUSHA. That's not true. I wasn't given time to put his good shirt on.

THE GOVERNOR'S WIFE. It must have been in a pigsty.

GRUSHA (*furiously*). I'm not a pig, but there are others who are. Where did you leave your child?

THE GOVERNOR'S WIFE. I'll show you, you vulgar creature! (*She is about to throw herself on Grusha, but is restrained by her Lawyers.*) She's a criminal, she must be whipped. Immediately!

THE SECOND LAWYER (*holding his hand over her mouth*). Gracious Natella Abashwili, you promised . . . Your Honor, the plaintiff's nerves . . .

AZDAK. Plaintiff and defendant! The Court has listened to your case, and has come to no decision as to who the real mother of this child is. I, as a judge, am obliged to choose a mother for the child. I'll make a test. Shauwa, get a piece of chalk and draw a circle on the floor. (*Shauwa does so.*) Now place the child in the center. (*Shauwa puts Michael, who smiles at Grusha, in the center of the circle.*) Stand next the circle, both of you. (*The Governor's Wife and Grusha step up to the circle.*) Now each of you take the child by one hand. (*They do so.*) The true mother is she who has the strength to pull the child out of the circle toward herself.

THE SECOND LAWYER (*quickly*). High Court of Justice, I object! The fate of the great Abashwili estates, which are bound to the child, as the heir, should not be made dependent on such a doubtful duel. In addition, my client does not command the strength of this person, who is accustomed to physical work.

AZDAK. She looks pretty well fed to me. Pull! (*The Governor's Wife pulls the child out of the circle on her side. Grusha has let go and stands aghast.*) What's the matter with you? You didn't pull!

GRUSHA. I didn't hold on to him.

THE FIRST LAWYER (*congratulating the Governor's Wife*). What did I say! The ties of blood!

GRUSHA (*running to Azdak*). Your Honor, I take back everything I said against you. I ask your forgiveness. If only I could keep him till he can speak all the words. He knows a few.

AZDAK. Don't influence the Court. I bet you only know twenty yourself. All right, I'll do the test once more, to make certain. (*The two women take up their positions again.*) Pull! (*Again Grusha lets go of the child.*)

GRUSHA (*in despair*). I brought him up! Am I to tear him to pieces? I can't do it!

AZDAK (*rising*). And in this manner the Court has established the true mother. (*To Grusha*) Take your child and be off. I advise you not to stay in the city with him. (*To the Governor's Wife*) And you disappear before I fine you for fraud. Your estates fall to the city. They'll be converted into a playground for children. They need one, and I've decided it shall be called after me: Azdak's Garden. (*The Governor's*

Wife has fainted and is carried out by the Lawyers and the Adjutant. Grusha stands motionless. Shauwa leads the child toward her.) Now I'll take off this judge's gown — it has grown too hot for me. I'm not cut out for a hero. In token of farewell I invite you all to a little dance outside on the meadow. Oh, I had almost forgotten something in my excitement . . . and that is, to sign the divorce decree.

(*Using the judge's chair as a table, he writes something on a piece of paper, and prepares to leave. Dance music has started.*)

SHAUWA (*having read what is on the paper*). But that's not right. You've not divorced the old people. You've divorced Grusha and her husband!

AZDAK. Have I divorced the wrong couple? What a pity! But it'll have to stand. I never retract! If I did, how could we keep order in our state? (*To the Old Couple*) But I'll invite you to my party instead. You don't mind dancing with each other, do you? (*To Grusha and Simon*) I've got forty piasters coming from *you.*

SIMON (*pulling out his purse*). That's cheap, Your Honor. And many thanks.

AZDAK (*pocketing the cash*). I'll need this.

GRUSHA (*to Michael*). So we'd better leave the city tonight, Michael? (*To Simon*) You like him?

SIMON. With my respects, I like him.

GRUSHA. And now I'll tell you: I took him because on that Easter Sunday, I got engaged to you. And so he's a child of love. Michael, let's dance.

(*She dances with Michael, Simon dances with the Cook, the Old Couple with each other. Azdak stands lost in thought. The dancers soon hide him from view. Occasionally he is seen, but less and less as more couples join the dance.*)

THE STORY TELLER.

    And after that evening Azdak disappeared and
      was not seen again.
    The people of Grusinia did not forget him but
      long remembered

The period of his judging as a brief golden age
Almost an age of justice.

(*All the couples dance off. Azdak has disappeared.*)

But you, you who have listened to the Story of the Chalk Circle,
Take note what men of old concluded:
That what there is shall go to those who are good for it,
Thus: the children to the motherly, that they prosper
The carts to good drivers, that they are well driven
And the valley to the waterers, that it bring forth fruit.

NOTES

The English versions in this book were made from German manuscripts which may not exactly correspond with future German editions of the plays. Smudges, errors, and other obscurities prevented us from making anything that could be called "definitive" versions. On the other hand, we did not presume to "adapt" our texts. We tried to write English that actors can speak while remaining as close to the original as possible. Since our versions of both plays were used in production before this book went to press, we were able to eliminate "unspeakable" lines and, in general, make sure that these parables are "for the theater."

Our intentions being so practical, it might seem that we ought here to supply detailed production notes. But for the almost prohibitive present cost of printing, we would probably have done so. As it is, we refer the reader to descriptions of Brecht's "epic" style in the New Directions edition of his *Private Life of the Master Race*, Mordecai Gorelik's *New Theatres for Old*, and Eric Bentley's *Playwright as Thinker*. Better than reading books, of course, is to see any production in which Brecht himself has had a hand: today this would mean a visit to Zürich, but not long ago many of us learned much from the Charles Laughton version of *Galileo* in Los Angeles and New York. There is little doubt, however, that amateurs might profitably approach the plays quite naively, staging them as they think fit. A few tips may here be in order.

Neither in its subject matter nor its style does "The Good Woman of Setzuan" invite a completely Chinese mode of production. The city of Setzuan is half-Westernized, and so should the production be. Otherwise the play will be "cute" after the fashion of recent pseudo-Chinese pieces.

"The Caucasian Chalk Circle" is not so immense a production problem as it seems. The four or five chorus members, besides sitting on the stage with the Story Teller, can play some of the other roles. The number of actors need not be anything like as large as the number of parts: the Governor of One, 1, and the Peasant of One, 3, can be played by the same actor; so can Lavrenti of Part One and the Bandit of Part Two; the Fat Woman (One, 1), the Peasant Woman (One, 2), and the Sister-in-law (One, 3) can be played by the same actress; and so on. The playing of several roles by one actor is the more feasible because the play should not be realistically presented. Symbolic masks might be used. The backgrounds can be projected on screens. Costume designers and makeup men might take hints from some of Bruegel's paintings. The whole must be simple.

It is possible, but not essential, for the Story Teller and Azdak to be the same actor. This procedure might make clear that Part One presents Grusha directly or, if you choose, from the viewpoint of the Story Teller; whereas in Part Two the whole thing turns round, and we see her from the viewpoint of society, symbolized by the law. In the German version of the play, however, the Story Teller *sings* his lines: it would be hard to find an actor who can adequately represent both a peasant ballad singer and Azdak.

E. B. and M. B.